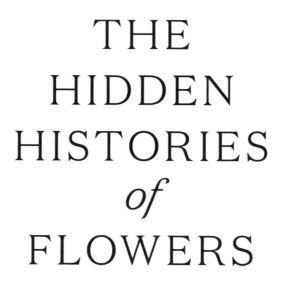

THE
HIDDEN
HISTORIES
of
FLOWERS

THE HIDDEN HISTORIES

of

FLOWERS

Fascinating Stories of Flora

Maddie & Alice Bailey

Hardie Grant

BOOKS

Introduction

The history of flowers and our relationship with them is fascinating and diverse, spanning centuries, countries, cultures and people. Flowers play an important part in historical tales, myths and legends, and continue to be studied scientifically so that we can discover more about their complex structure and properties, and how we can use them and learn from them. Having cut flowers in the home is a way to bring nature closer to us, and we gift them to communicate some of the more difficult emotions we experience without having to use words, so it's no surprise that they are so beloved.

While people treasure the beauty of this natural commodity, it's important to also remember that flowers serve a very real purpose to the plants that produce them, and that they are a product of thousands of years of evolution. Flowers are essential to the survival of all living things on planet Earth, and without them, life as we know it would not exist.

If, like us, you find yourself wondering about the deeper meanings behind flowers and are keen to explore their inner workings and place in history, this book is a good place to start.

Because the world of flowers is so vast and captivating, we found it very difficult to pick just one area to explore. Instead, we decided to look into a broad range of topics, to let you decide which you'd like to explore further and in which direction to continue your journey into the fascinating world of flowers.

Where do flowers come from and how do they end up in our homes? What exactly is the difference between a weed and a wildflower? Over the following pages, we explore the symbolism and meaning behind flowers and how these have evolved over time. We also look at the way humans interact with flowers based on cultural and geographical differences, and we consider how flowers have been coveted for their medicinal aspects as well as for their visual merits. We discover which common flowers can be used in cooking, and how some with a darker side have been used as murderous tools. We find out how such a readily available commodity has become a luxury for some while it remains a mainstay of everyday life for others, and we even explore the modern-day flower industry as we take you on a tour of wholesalers, growers and an auction house in the Netherlands.

While this book spans different countries and cultures, it's important to note that we have approached our research and writing from the perspective of our homes in the UK, where the seasons and growing conditions may differ to yours. Having worked with flowers for most of our lives, we're familiar with those from our own country as well as those native to others, but for the most part, we have chosen to spotlight flowers from our homeland that mean something to us. We hope that some of these flowers are familiar to you, and if they are not, that you can discover a new flower to fall in love with.

CHAPTER 1

FLOWERS
IN LORE

FAIRY TALES
AND MYTHOLOGY

As difficult as it is to imagine a world without flowers, it is similarly difficult to imagine a fairy tale or mythical story in which flowers are absent. The tale of Red Riding Hood wouldn't be nearly as intriguing and mystical without its forest full of bluebells and foxgloves, and the Brothers Grimm and Hans Christian Andersen would have had a much harder time telling their stories without the symbolism of the ever-present rose.

Similarly, many Greek and Roman myths are centred around flowers, and many of the botanical names for flowers have been inspired by characters that appear in mythology (think Narcissus, Hyacinthus and Iris). It is not just Greek and Roman myths, either – flowers are present in mythical tales from every country, culture and religion across the globe. Flowers are used in these myths and stories to symbolise everything from love and death to deception, innocence, beauty and pain.

In Britain, the Victorians used flowers symbolically, too, notably in artworks, and also when gifting them. They created floriography, or the 'language of flowers', which is still used by many today, whether consciously or subconsciously.

Bluebells

Native Location
United Kingdom

Hyacinthoides non-scripta, commonly known as the bluebell, is a quintessentially British bulb that can be found growing in woodlands across the British Isles. Although bluebells grow in countries across much of Western Europe, they are most densely populated in the UK, and have become an emblem of the English countryside. It is said that bluebells can only be found growing naturally in ancient woodland, and so to find them growing is to walk through history – in fact, the Woodland Trust says that to contain naturalised bluebells, a wooded area must be at least five centuries old. It is no wonder, then, that they are so deeply ingrained in the fairy tales and myths of Britain.

IN FAIRY TALES AND FOLKLORE

When we think of bluebells, we are transported to bucolic scenes: bluebells growing by the gate of a solitary thatched cottage surrounded by wildflowers, or blooming stems sprinkled through the mossy earth of a shaded clearing in a wood, surrounded by cool, undisturbed air. Or you may connect more to the image of steep, tree-filled banks lining a winding country road, the glints of blue flashing by as you drive through the dappled sunlight. Whatever picture is conjured up for you, the idea of a bluebell is enchanting.

In Victorian floriography, bluebells were said to symbolise kindness and humility, which is perhaps why they are so often associated with the innocence and naivety of youth. But conversely, British folklore also suggests that the existence of bluebells in ancient woodland confirms the presence of fairies – the most mischievous of all the mythical creatures. It was said that when the fairy folk wanted to call their kin to meetings or festivities, they would ring the bluebells in order to 'call the fae forth' – and if any human should be unfortunate enough to bear witness to the sound, misfortune (and by some accounts, even death) would follow soon after. As for those who were foolish enough to pick a bluebell from the forest floor, the angered fairy folk were said to enchant the picker and lead them astray, leaving them to wander, lost, for days, if not months, afterwards. Children who would play among, trample or gather bluebells from the forest were subject to the worst fate – they would be kidnapped by the fairy folk, never to be seen again. The children's rhyme 'In and out the dusting bluebells', is said to be a song made in reference to this myth.

THE ONE NOT WRITTEN ABOUT

The bluebell's Latin botanical name, *Hyacinthoides non-scripta*, can be roughly translated as 'the plant that looks like a hyacinth but is not written about'. While this sounds a little clumsy, Swedish botanist Carl Linnaeus, the father of taxonomy, named the bulb this so that it would not be confused with the famous hyacinth written about in Greek mythology.

As with many Greek myths, the tale of Hyacinthus is one of tragedy. Hyacinthus was a Spartan prince, and his beauty radiated so far and wide that it caught the attention of the god, Apollo, who fell instantly in love with the youth. Hyacinthus' beauty also attracted Zephyrus, the god of the west wind, but the prince chose Apollo over any other suitors and the two spent much of their time together. One day, during a game of quoits, Apollo threw his discus a great distance. The jealous Zephyrus saw his chance and blew the discus off course with such force that it hit Hyacinthus in the head, killing him instantly. Overcome with grief, Apollo held the deceased Hyacinthus in his arms, and in a bid to immortalise his lover, he turned the blood that fell from the prince and on to the ground into a flower, with the words 'AI, AI' (an exclamation meaning 'alas') inscribed on its petals.

"Against a dark sky,
all flowers look like
fireworks. There is
something strange about
them, at once vivid and
secret, like flowers traced
in fire in the phantasmal
garden of a witch."

—

G.K. Chesterton,
writer

Foxgloves

Native Location
Europe

The famous foxglove (*Digitalis*) has enchanted communities for centuries and sits at the centre of many folk and fairy tales. Both the plant's botanical and common names allude to its place in folk-lore and are linked to the foxglove's tubular, mitten-like flowers, which appear in its second year of growth. There is much debate surrounding the origin of the plant's common and Latin names, but many accounts suggest the common name 'foxglove' is derived from an older name given to the plant, 'folk's glove', which refers to fairy folk rather than foxes. Its botanical name, *Digitalis*, means 'of the fingers' in Latin, and is thought to come from the German common name for the plant, *Fingerhut*, which means 'thimble'.

By some accounts, however, the 'glove' part of the plant's name actually comes from the Anglo-Saxon word *gliew*, which was the name given to an instrument covered in bells. By this reckoning, the common name for the plant actually means 'fairy bells'. This could make sense, as foxgloves were certainly said to be revered by the nefarious fairy folk. Indeed, the presence of foxgloves supposedly indicates the presence of fairies, and the swaying of a foxglove in the wind was often thought to be a subtle nod or bow to a passing fairy. Some tales even suggested that the magical beings lived within the flowers, making it bad luck to pick a foxglove flower – anyone who did so would anger the fairy folk and have curses bestowed upon them.

In Victorian floriography, these striking, bell-like blooms represent insincerity – but also immortality.

MISCHIEVOUS MITTENS

While many creatures allegedy used foxglove flowers to cause mischief, according to myth and legend, it was foxes that used them the most (this could be the reason the plant became known as a foxglove in the first place, although some believe it was so named due to the mishearing of 'folk's glove'). Fairies were said to give the flowers to foxes, and these floral mittens allowed the foxes either to become totally invisible or simply incredibly stealthy. This meant that foxes could butcher chickens in their coops, steal eggs from hens and even elude the malicious fox hunter. In all folkloric tales surrounding the plant, the flowers are used as gloves to enhance power or to enable the wearer to complete mischievous deeds.

JUNO AND MARS

Unsurprisingly, the foxglove also appears in ancient myths. In Roman mythology, Juno is the goddess of childbirth and marriage. When her husband, Jupiter, spontaneously gave birth to the goddess Minerva from his head, without the need for a mother, Juno was angered. In order to exact her revenge, Juno gave birth to the war god Mars, this time without the need for a father. She was helped in this deed by Flora, the goddess of spring and flowers, who stroked Juno with a foxglove flower in order to induce pregnancy.

Daisies

Native Location
Europe

Daisies (*Bellis perennis*) are unassuming flowers and, perhaps because they grow so easily and in such large clusters, they are often overlooked by those who are old enough to have lost interest in the more mundane aspects of the natural world. Mostly found growing among grass in lawns or on sunny, barren banks, the more meticulous gardener may think of them as a nuisance, but to others, they signal the beginning of spring. Daisies seem to be most loved by children, who make daisy chains and pluck petals from the flowers. Perhaps it is because of this that in Victorian floriography, they represent innocence, purity, love and rebirth.

Daisies have even been used to predict the future: by plucking the petals from the flower head one by one and uttering the words 'he loves me, he loves me not', young people have been able to predict whether or not their romantic interest is in love with them, how long it will be until they get married, and even what occupation their future spouse will have.

The common name 'daisy' originates from the Old English *daeges eage* (day's eye), which refers to the fact that the flower opens up in the sunshine.

IN MYTH AND LEGEND

The botanical name for the plant comes from Roman mythology. Belides, a woodland nymph, was found frolicking in a wooded area with other nymphs when Vertumnus, the god of seasons and orchards, spotted her and fell in love. Eager to escape his advances, Belides turned herself in to a daisy, and it is from this that we get the genus *Bellis*.

The ancient Celts, on the other hand, believed that daisies were a flower that showed sympathy from the gods. If a baby was stillborn or died during infancy, the appearance of daisies on the grave was seen as a gift from the gods to ease the pain of the mourning parents.

LUCK, SUPERSTITION
AND THE OCCULT

Flowers, trees and other plants are deeply rooted in the worlds of superstition and the occult. From lucky heather sold by travellers to the silence demanded by a monkey puzzle tree, we've all heard one tale or another about plants evoking or disrupting good fortune.

Of course, superstitions and folklore are often the result of tales being passed down and gradually embellished over generations, and every country, culture and religion will have different ideas of what is lucky or unlucky, and what is associated with the devil, ill health, the occult, witches, joy, fertility, love, friendship and so on. Many plant-based superstitions and tales are rooted in scientific principles, however, and as scientific study advances, these ideas become much easier to explain. The medicinal benefits of a particular plant, for example – though not fully understood at the time – may have caused ancient communities to label that plant as 'lucky', while plants that resulted in sickness or even death when consumed or improperly prepared may have been considered 'unlucky' or 'cursed'.

Hawthorn

Native Location
Northern Europe

Hawthorn (*Crataegus*), like many shrubs that blossom in May, has long been considered unlucky in the home. Even today, those living in the countryside who remember the old superstitions won't allow their children to bring the blossoms inside. The reasons for this span centuries, and as with many superstitions, they stem from a fear of disease and death.

Some speculate that the idea that hawthorn blossoms invite bad luck began in Britain during the plague-ravaged medieval period. The stems were often brought into the home to mask the stench of accumulating corpses, and eventually became associated with the smell of death. It doesn't help that once hawthorn blossoms begin to die, they produce a rancid-smelling chemical called trimethylamine, which makes them smell like rotting flesh. Those who had brought the blooms in to mask the scent of the dead worried that they'd somehow been infused with the plague. It may have been this, coupled with the fact that the plant's bright red, blood-coloured berries follow the foul-smelling blossom, that made people believe that bringing the blossoms inside was to invite the plague itself.

In Ireland, hawthorn is equally shrouded in superstition. Wild hawthorn is considered sacred and magical, and so many farmers leave fields of hawthorn undisturbed in an attempt to avoid summoning bad luck by uprooting it.

Before the 20th century (and to a lesser extent nowadays), Hawthorn was especially popular during the Irish May festival Lá Bealtaine (Beltane), which is nestled on the calendar between the spring equinox and summer solstice, and marks the beginning of summer (similar to other May Day festivals). 'May bushes', including the infamous hawthorn, would be in full bloom at that time and were said to protect homes and towns from the mischievous deeds of fairy folk, who were particularly active during the festivities. Historically, townsfolk would parade through the streets with a hawthorn bush to decorate in order to appease the *aos sí* (Irish mythological creatures similar to fairies or elves, who are descendants of fallen angels or another supernatural race) and would decorate their porches and the outsides of their homes with wreaths made from hawthorn to keep bad luck at bay.

Hawthorn also coincides with the Irish festival Oíche Shamhna (Halloween). Around this time, the plant undergoes a striking transformation, its pale white springtime blossoms replaced with deep red, shiny berries, like a blood-coloured moth emerging from a decaying cocoon. These blossom and berry transformations coinciding with two of the most important festivals in Irish history is surely part of the reason the hawthorn is both feared and respected throughout the country.

Elderflowers

Native Location
Europe

Depending on where you look, the elder (*Sambucus nigra*) and its flowers have either been recorded as a symbol of good luck, fertility and a means to ward off evil, or their name has been tarnished by association with bad luck, curses, the occult and devilry.

Since the shrub itself is so ancient – it has existed in the British Isles and much of Europe for centuries – the superstitions surrounding elder are both numerous and extremely muddled, with much of the confusion seeming to coincide with the rise of Christianity and the overthrow of paganism.

Druids, pagans and others following ancient pre-Christian beliefs from across the world suggested that the tree was a symbol of good luck. The tree's wood, flowers and berries were seen as a gift from the Earth Mother (the personification of the Earth and the natural world, a deity like Gaia) – some followers even speculated that she lived inside of it. The Earth Mother was highly respected among these communities, and those who worshipped her believed that to disregard her would result in bad luck. Because of this, it became known that elder should not be cut without permission from the Earth Mother residing inside the plant first, lest the chopper suffer the consequences (in Romania, for example, the punishment was toothache). Anybody hoping to use the wood of the elder should therefore ask the elder for permission, then wait for permission to be granted by the silence of the plant before being free to use it. If permission was not given (or asked for), any furniture or tools made with the wood and brought inside the home would bestow bad luck on the house and its occupants. Even worse, if a cradle or cot was made from the stolen elder, any child or baby placed inside it would be relentlessly taunted and grabbed at by the spirit of the plant.

During the Middle Ages in Britain, elder was planted on or near to gravesites and in cemeteries as a way of ensuring a peaceful rest for the dead. It was thought that when an elder planted over a grave flowered, it indicated that the soul of the occupant was at peace and had passed over to the other side. Perhaps due to the rise in Christianity and subsequent diminishing of pagan beliefs in many places, elder was also planted close to the home to ward off evil spirits, witches, or the devil and to promote fertility. Contrary to this idea, some people believed that rather than elder providing protection from them, witches could actually turn themselves into elder trees, and that they used elder wood to make their magic wands and broomsticks.

Burning elder was also considered by some as a guaranteed way to raise the devil. Elder is fairly difficult to burn, and many saw the diminishing of a fire after elder was added as a sign of bad luck. If the fire sustained, the screaming and spitting caused by the sap of the wood was seen as a release of demons and black magic. If the fire sustained for long enough to cook a meal, the resulting food was considered poisonous and unfit for consumption. Of course, we now know that the composition of the wood and its sap is the reason why the wood isn't suited to burning. The wood also contains cyanide and other toxic chemicals that result in a foul-smelling smoke – another probable reason why many people saw the burning of elder as a release of evil.

Deadly Nightshade

Native Locations
Europe, North Africa
and Western Asia

Atropa belladonna, more commonly known as deadly nightshade or belladonna, is one of the most poisonous plants to ever have graced the British Isles. Due to its deadly nature, there are plenty of superstitions surrounding the plant, most of which involve cults, witches and the devil.

The plant's botanical name does a good job of providing some context for the plant's associations. Its genus, *Atropa*, refers to Atropos, one of the three Fates of Greek mythology. The fates were collectively responsible for weaving, measuring and snipping the mortal thread. Atropos, the eldest of the Fates, had the job of cutting the thread with her sharpened scissors, choosing how and when to end the life of a mortal. This nod to the most formidable Fate alludes to the deadly nature of the plant and its ability to cut short the mortal thread at any time.

Belladonna, the plant's species name, is derived from a much more seductive use of the plant. Meaning 'beautiful woman' in Italian, it refers to the cosmetic use of the berries during the Renaissance period. Women during this era dilated their pupils using eye drops made from a concoction containing the juice of deadly nightshade berries in order to feign the appearance of arousal. This trend is demonstrated in paintings from the time, as the artists would often ask models to dilate their pupils for sittings. Of course, this allure came at great personal risk, with women suffering from vision loss as well as a rapid heart rate and early signs of poisoning. Many opticians still use atropine eye drops to dilate the pupils of patients before surgery today.

It isn't only the toxicity of the plant that has informed its reputation. According to ancient lore, all deadly nightshade plants belong to the devil, who spends every night (apart from the witches' sabbath) tending to them. Those who eat the berries without permission are therefore punished by death, and parents often told children that if they ate the berries they would meet the devil.

Throughout history, deadly nightshade has been used by cults, shamans and witches to induce trance-like states. In ancient Greece, maenads, who were the female followers of the god Dionysus (the god of wine, revelry, madness and ecstasy), were said to have drunk a concoction containing deadly nightshade, consumed alcohol and taken other drugs while dancing, screaming and flailing around to induce a state of lunacy, at which point their souls would leave their bodies and give them the ability to communicate freely with Dionysus.

Shamans and witches were also said to use concoctions made from deadly nightshade to invoke divination and astral projection. Witches during the medieval period, for example, were said to prepare ointments and salves using the berries of the plant, often paired with monkshood (page 92), hemlock and mandrake (all incredibly poisonous plants). The plants were combined with oil or fat to reduce the toxicity of the concoction, and then rubbed into the skin, which would enable flight to other places and realms where they could convene with other witches, demons and even the devil. However, since the alkaloids within plants like deadly nightshade (most notably atropine) induce severe, peyote-like hallucinations and delirium, and those who have been poisoned by the plant have reported feeling as though they were flying, the chances are that the trance-like state that the witches fell into merely caused them to *believe* that they'd achieved flight.

CHAPTER 2

A LIFESTYLE
OR A LUXURY?
– COUNTRIES'
RELATIONSHIPS
WITH FLOWERS

Mexico

When thinking of flowers in Mexico, there's no doubt that for most of us, it's the vibrant arrangements that decorate the *ofrendas* (altars) during the Day of the Dead celebrations that spring to mind. But flowers aren't just used for religious ceremonies and festivals in Mexico – they're a hugely important part of daily life that is deeply ingrained in the culture. Because of the diverse climate across the country, there are a wide variety of tropical plants and flowers in season at any given time of year, and the people of Mexico are generally very passionate about making the most of them. Anyone with access to a garden or outdoor space will likely be growing a mix of cacti, succulents, tropical palms, roses, calendula and many more plants depending on the region and local climate. In regions such as Oaxaca (a subtropical climate), many flowers bloom all year round, including bougainvillaea, which is a firm favourite grown by many households. If flowers from a household's own crop are not available, they will be bought from the local *tianguis* (food and produce markets), which offer tables full of locally grown and seasonal flowers being sold by nearby small-scale growers. Because flowers are so readily available, they are seen not as a luxury afforded by the few, but as a nationwide resource to be enjoyed by the masses.

But as much as flowers are a part of everyday life in Mexico, they are, of course, absolutely essential for special occasions. When buying extravagant gift arrangements or flowers for events and festivities, it is now increasingly common to buy from commercial flower shops or large-scale markets such as the famous Mercado Jamaica (hibiscus market) in Mexico City. As well as stocking flowers grown across the country, these sellers also have access to blooms from specialist growers across the globe – from the glasshouses of the Netherlands to the rose farms of Colombia and Kenya. The array of choice is necessary, as many special occasions have specific

flowers or colours associated with them. Religious ceremonies, festivals, weddings and funerals all have their own symbolic flowers with significant meanings behind them.

THE DAY OF THE DEAD
AND SYMBOLIC FLOWERS

The Day of the Dead (Día de Muertos) is a huge occasion for flowers and one that showcases their symbolism well. It is a particularly prominent celebration in Mexico, in which past family members are honoured and their spirits are freed to visit the world of the living and be reunited with loved ones. Families come together on this day to create an *ofrenda* which is dressed with decorations, candles, food, tequila or mezcal, photographs and personal items of the deceased, as well as an abundance of brightly coloured and wonderfully scented flowers. The scent of the flowers on this occasion is just as important as the vibrant colours: they help to guide the souls of deceased family members to the altar prepared for them, and also bring them the joy and pleasures of the life they once experienced. Hot pinks, reds, bright yellows and oranges adorn the altars and are used alongside white flowers to create floral arches, garlands, wreaths, crucifixes and stars. Among these, there is one flower that is by far the most popular choice for the Day of the Dead – the African or Mexican marigold (*Tagetes erecta*).

Known in Mexico as *cempasúchil* ('flower of 400 petals or lives') or *flor de muertos* ('flower of the dead'), these large marigolds provide both the vibrancy and fragrance to attract souls. As well as using the flowers on tombs, altars and graves, families in smaller towns will often scatter marigold petals to form a path from the cemetery to their front doors to lead the dead home. In larger towns, where this might not be possible, a petal pathway from the front door of a home to the altar within is common. The petals of the marigold are also thought to possess cleansing properties and are often arranged in the form of a cross on the floor in front of the altar so the souls may be cleansed of their sins when they tread upon them.

Another flower of significance for the Day of the Dead is the cockscomb (*Celosia argentea var. cristata*), also known as red velvet (*terciopelo rojo*). These flowers, which look like a fuzzy brain or complex sea coral, are available in many colours, but the colour most widely used for the Day of the Dead is deep red. This not only adds to the rich colour of floral arrangements, but is also symbolic of the blood of Christ and resurrection from the dead.

Gladioli are another key flower that are used for their symbolic meaning. They represent remembrance and faithfulness, but are likely to be a popular choice among florists for their tall and structured form as well as their significance. Their striking shape adds a beautiful contrast and diversity of shape when arranged beside the low and wide heads of marigolds and cockscomb.

Although warm and inviting colours are key for this celebration, you will frequently find white flowers (in particular *Chrysanthemum × morifolium*) tucked in alongside them. While white flowers are most commonly associated with weddings and funerals in Mexico, their symbolism is actually very fitting for the Day of the Dead, as they represent peace, beauty and sympathy. The tuberose (*Polianthes tuberosa*), although not necessarily a common choice for Day of the Dead ceremonies, is a great example of a white flower that carries both symbolic meaning and a beautiful scent. These flowers are tall and elegant, with trumpets of small white flowers edged in soft pink extending from a single stem. This small splash of colour proves useful in helping the white flowers to blend in with colourful ones. Their delightful scent, not dissimilar to the smell of jasmine (*Jasminum officinale*), is perfect for guiding spirits home, bringing decadence to a graveside or giving a bride something joyous to smell while walking down the aisle.

MEXICO AND THE CALLA LILY

When it comes to white flowers, the one most heavily associated with Mexican culture is the calla or arum lily (*Zantedeschia aethiopica*). There is no symbolism associated with this flower – it is simply admired for its understated elegance and beauty, both in Mexico and across the globe. It was particularly favoured by artists in the early 20th century, including one of Mexico's most prolific painters, Diego Rivera. Rivera seemed to have a particular fascination with the calla lily and featured it in many of his murals. It is largely thanks to his works that the calla lily has become so significant in Mexican culture and folk art. Some of his favourite subjects were the indigenous people of Mexico, and his depictions of their day-to-day life often featured female vendors selling the lilies. There has been plenty of speculation about why the flower features so heavily in his works, but the general consensus is that the calla lily was used as a way to celebrate indigenous labour, customs and life. Rivera's wife and fellow artist, Frida Kahlo, also played an important role in the popularity of the flower. Although she only featured it in a few of her self-portraits, it became associated with her image, further catapulting the flower to fame.

Although the flower isn't native to Mexico – it is believed to have been brought to Mexico during the country's colonisation – it now grows prolifically in the temperate climates of the country. There are, however, over 20 plants from the same family (Araceae) that are native to Mexico and similar in appearance, with a trumpet-shaped 'petal' known as a spathe (a type of bract, which is a modified leaf) surrounding a phallic-looking spike (spadix), which is covered with tiny flowers. These native flowers feature heavily in pre-Columbian art and might be another reason why Rivera featured them so frequently.

The calla lily is now used nationwide for weddings and funerals: for weddings because it represents innocence, sensuality and purity, and also because the shape of the 'petal' is reminiscent of a wedding dress; and for funerals because it represents rebirth, revolution and resurrection. Regardless of the calla lily's symbolic meaning to the people of Mexico today, its rise to popular use through the historic art of the country is deeply significant.

"I paint flowers
so they will not die."

—

Frida Kahlo,
artist

Russia

Russia is one of the biggest flower-buying nations in the world, and a glance into the country's tradition of gifting flowers quickly demonstrates why. There is a huge gifting culture in Russia, and whether you're visiting someone's home, going on a date or simply haven't seen a friend for a while, the expectation is that you will bring flowers. Flowers are used to express affection, gratitude, congratulations, commiserations and everything in between. If you're living in Russia and enjoy going out to see friends or having guests over, you'll probably have a bunch of flowers in your home. Even during the Soviet era when the importation of goods was minimal and private business was banned, the selling of flowers was an exception to the rule as they were considered such an essential part of social convention.

FLOWERS IN THE SOVIET UNION

Although the sale of flowers was somewhat exempt from the economic rules of the Soviet Union, it was still regulated. Buying imported flowers was considered a real luxury, and the shops that sold them were few and far between, often selling old stock that wasn't particularly fresh. However, it was still acceptable to sell or exchange 'excess produce' from your garden. This term was incredibly flexible and, as it turns out, flowers were grown for profit not just in people's gardens, but on the land of their *dachas* (country holiday homes) and in small-scale greenhouses across the country. These flowers were then sold at markets, on makeshift street-side stands, outside train and metro stations and at petrol (gas) stations, operating all year round and often open 24/7. Wherever you were, you wouldn't have to go far to find someone selling flowers, whether it be a semi-professional growing for profit or an old lady selling directly from her garden.

While it seems there was no real problem buying flowers during the Soviet era, availability was mostly limited by the seasons and whatever would grow locally, and it was near impossible to buy an 'exotic' flower arrangement. It may be that the lack of availability during this period has contributed to the abundance of imported flowers being bought and sold across Russia today.

THE LANGUAGE OF FLOWERS AND THE ART OF GIFTING

Take a walk down a busy Russian street, and you'll likely glimpse a flower shop or street vendor within seconds – and probably a few of their customers carrying bunches down the street, too. But when is it appropriate to give flowers? Well… always! If in doubt when going anywhere in Russia, take flowers, but be sure to brush up on the local flower-gifting etiquette beforehand to avoid an unintentional faux pas.

Firstly, it's worth noting that flowers are a gift typically reserved for women, although it isn't unusual to buy a man flowers when marking a significant occasion such as an important birthday. It is also customary to offer older women, perhaps a couple of generations above your own, a flowering potted plant. However, this is something that should be avoided for the younger generation unless you know for sure which flowers they like, as having potted plants can be quite a commitment.

There are also a number of more nuanced rules that all Russians grow up knowing, but might catch a foreigner off guard:

- Even numbers are reserved for funerals or commiserations. If you're buying flowers for any kind of happy occasion, then you must always purchase an odd number. While this is often supposedly ignored in larger bouquets, it is still a frequent request in flower shops to make sure big bunches use odd numbers. That means a dozen roses are out of the picture for romantic gestures – go for thirteen instead.

- If you're looking for love, avoid red carnations. They're probably the least romantic flower as they're associated with Soviet holidays and seen as a revolutionary flower.

- Another thing to remember if you're giving flowers to a date is that colour matters. As a general rule, the brighter the flowers, the stronger your feelings – particularly with roses. For a first date, start with a white or pale-coloured rose and work your way up towards red as a sign that your love is deepening. Alternatively, avoid roses altogether and find out her favourite seasonal flowers to gift instead – just make sure to avoid yellow.

- Yellow flowers are a symbol of sadness, deceit and, most importantly, an impending break-up – so don't give your date a big yellow bouquet!

KEY FLOWER-GIVING OCCASIONS

Although it's common to see people carrying flowers on any given day, there are some occasions in Russia when you can be sure that the flower shops and markets will be full to the brim with people picking out bunches, and you'll be lucky to make it through the sea of customers without queueing for hours.

Many of Russia's major flower-buying holidays are common to those elsewhere in the world, for example Valentine's Day, Mother's Day and Christmas. There are a couple of occasions, however, that go above and beyond these in the sheer quantity of flowers bought and sold.

8 March, International Women's Day
Although Valentine's Day is celebrated in Russia, it's considered by many as a token holiday that is overbearingly romantic and westernised. International Women's Day, however, encompasses the broad range of ways that women should be appreciated and applies

to all the women in someone's life as opposed to just their romantic partner. In Russia, both men and women will give bunches to their mothers, sisters, daughters, co-workers, wives and girlfriends, so it's no surprise that International Women's Day typically accounts for around 10 per cent of the country's total annual flower income. Traditionally, scented flowering mimosa (*Acacia dealbata*), which is at the height of its season in March, was the flower of choice, but since the reintroduction of imported flowers this is no longer the case (it could also have something to do with the fact that the flowers are yellow). Now the favourite flower is the rose. One flower seller with 13 shops across Moscow exclusively selling imported roses was reported to have sold about 150,000 stems of roses on International Women's Day – the amount he would usually sell in a month.

1 September, Knowledge Day

Knowledge Day, which is the first day back at school, is a day of celebration in Russia. Children dress smartly in their uniforms, ceremonies take place (such as a boy from the final year carrying a first-year girl on his shoulders while she rings the new year bell) and flowers are gifted. Every child in every year group will bring a bouquet for their teacher, and the bouquets are often crafted from a glorious array of extravagant flowers. Traditionally, bouquets should include gladioli and asters (three of the former and five of the latter), but nowadays if people choose to include these flowers, they're often arranged alongside roses, chrysanthemums and carnations, to name a few. While there is no particular tradition around the colour of arrangements, using red gladioli is typical. A classroom filled with as many bouquets as children is sure to bring a joyous start to the new school year and is a fantastic show of appreciation to the teachers, who probably receive more flowers than they know what to do with.

"Flowers always make people better, happier and more helpful; they are sunshine, food and medicine for the soul."

—

Luther Burbank,
American botanist

The United Kingdom

You only have to peek into the gardens of British homes to understand the nation's passion for flowers. As a country, the UK is known for its love of gardening, perhaps more so than any other nation, and although its popularity comes in waves, the cut flower industry is continuing to grow. Those with gardens might cut their own flowers to take inside, but those without an outside space will always find somewhere nearby to buy from – hopefully a flower shop or local florist rather than a supermarket. However important flowers are to the UK as a nation, though, there is a tendency to overlook them for the everyday and instead to go all out for big life events, such as births, romantic declarations, marriages and deaths. This may be because of the UK's history of floriography, or the 'language of flowers'.

Floriography has been practised for thousands of years across many different cultures, but it became extremely popular in Britain during the Victorian era. It was one of the most commonly enjoyed hobbies of the time, allowing people to convey a novel's worth of meaning through the use of specific combinations of flowers in a bouquet. This was particularly useful for the middle and upper classes of society, who were otherwise bound by strict etiquette and social conventions. Much of this language has since become obsolete, but there are still echoes of Victorian floriography resonating in the flowers gifted in the UK today. Red roses remain the most popular choice as a symbol of love, as they were traditionally associated with Venus, the goddess of love. White lilies (*Lilium candidum*), conveying innocence and purity, are often the first pick for funeral arrangements. Lily of the valley (*Convallaria majalis*), carrying the same meanings as white lilies but with trustworthiness and happiness added to the sentiment, are a go-to for weddings.

Perhaps it comes as no surprise that British people use flowers as a way of conveying emotions. The nation has the reputation

of being tight-lipped, and giving flowers is the perfect way to communicate feelings that would otherwise be hard to express in words. This is something that's particularly true of the male population when expressing love. Luckily for them, Valentine's Day is one of the country's biggest flower-giving occasions by far.

KEY FLOWER-GIVING OCCASIONS

We are a nation of traditionalists when it comes to the exchanging of flowers, so having a set list of dates to do so suits us very well indeed. Although taking flowers to the homes of our friends and families is nowadays often disregarded in favour of a bottle of wine, there are two occasions in the calendar that even those with modern tendencies regularly adhere to.

14 February, Valentine's Day
Valentine's Day has a long history. St Valentine was a priest in ancient Rome who was beheaded by Emperor Claudius II on 14 February for helping Christian couples to wed while the religion was banned. While some believe Valentine's Day is celebrated on this date to commemorate his execution, there are theories that the Christian Church started the Feast of St Valentine to overshadow the pagan fertility festival, Lupercalia, which took place on 15 February. Either way, it wasn't until much later that this saint's name was strongly associated with love. The English poet Geoffrey Chaucer was the first to romanticise the now-infamous February date by linking it with the springtime mating season in his poem *Parlement of Foules*, written in around 1382. Even then, it wasn't until the 17th century that Valentine's Day flowers became tradition, and it took until the Victorian era before it became big business to send cards and give flowers.

Today, Valentine's Day is an important part of British flower-giving culture, even among those who are not avid celebrators of the holiday. Many who have no real interest in marking the occasion will still take a few flowers home for their significant other. In recent years, there has been a backlash against the saint's day, as people have come to believe it is an occasion borne from the marketing schemes of commercial card companies. While its rise in popularity can certainly be linked to big corporations, we must also acknowledge its deep-rooted place in British custom and the love language developed through flowers.

March (various dates), Mother's Day
Mother's Day is another occasion steeped in tradition, and for Brits, its one that's on par with Valentine's Day when it comes to the exchanging of cut flowers. Historically, young people in service were only granted one day off a year. This day in spring became known as Mothering Sunday. Youths would walk from their place of service back to their family home, gathering wildflowers for their mothers along the way. Even if the majority of us today are more likely to visit our local florist than go foraging in the fields, the practice of giving seasonal spring flowers is generally followed, and florists favour vibrant colours that bring with them the joys of the changing season. Mimosa (*Acacia dealbata*) is a firm favourite. Its vivid yellow, pom-pom-like flowers exude a glorious scent that conjures up images of a warm and sunny spring day. Tulips, ranunculus and hyacinths are also high on the list of most desired flowers for Mother's Day, each available in a vast array of delightful hues, from rich primary colours to soft pastel tones. Most florists will have a display full to the brim with wonderful, seasonal flowers and foliage to choose from, and what better way to show appreciation for your mother than to bring a bunch of spring joy to her home?

THE NATURE OF BUYING

In the UK, florists have always been there for big occasions and will be visited on any significant flower-buying event. But the way flowers are purchased on a more regular basis has changed. If people want to grab a bunch of flowers on the way home, the supermarket (grocery store) or petrol (gas) station forecourt might be the first port of call.

Up until the 1980s, the British flower industry was in full bloom, and florists and supermarkets alike could buy British-grown flowers at low prices. Now, the majority of flowers sold in Britain are imported, and with the cost of importation at an all-time high and expenses for Dutch growers rising, the price of flowers in local flower shops has increased. However, this isn't a change that's being reflected by supermarkets. They sell flowers as a loss leader – the name given to a sales strategy in which a product is sold at an unprofitable price to attract new customers or encourage sales of other items in store. Not only does this strategy set unrealistic expectations for customers, it takes business away from smaller tradespeople. What's more, supermarket bunches tend to consist of old flowers that have been treated with chemicals to make them last longer, have no scent, don't represent the changing seasons and are packaged in plastic. Such arrangements do not symbolise love, gratitude or other emotions in the way that local, seasonal flowers do.

Luckily, we are on the path of change once more, with the British flower industry on the rise. People are once more appreciating the value of locally sourced and seasonal produce, and society's bid to reduce its carbon footprint and air miles has changed our perspective on imported goods.

People are also increasingly finding their local florist to be a place where they can engage in the joys of the much-loved natural product they're buying, chatting with the florist about the flowers and where they've come from and building a relationship with someone who will get to know their style. Buying flowers from a florist is a much more mindful and intentional shopping experience than an impulse buy at the supermarket checkout. Flowers in a florist will always be more expensive than the supermarket, but we are learning once again to value scented, seasonal blooms at a more realistic cost. How much more beautiful is a small posy of peonies and nigella, a bunch of cornflowers, or the soft scent of sweet peas, than some generic yellow chrysanthemums bought out of season?

"Sing a song of seasons!
something bright in all!
flowers in the summer,
fires in the fall!"

—

Robert Louis Stevenson,
novelist

CHAPTER 3

WEEDS OR WILDFLOWERS?

THE CHANGING ATTITUDE TOWARDS WEEDS

Come springtime, the effects of winter start to wear off and early season rains begin to take hold. This is when you will see wildflowers and weeds sprouting up all over the place. In parks, on paved streets, on the sides of motorways (highways) and in gardens and yards. But what is the difference between a weed and a wildflower? In many cases, it simply comes down to preferences – what is considered a weed by one person may be a much-welcomed wildflower to others.

People's feelings about weeds have fluctuated greatly over time, with ancient civilisations coveting them as a source of medicine but the modern gardener loathing them for their appearance in manicured lawns and meticulously designed flower beds. Despite the modern attitude, it appears that weeds have made a comeback, featuring heavily in the narrative and gardens of the Chelsea Flower Show 2023, where they were hailed as heroes for their huge benefits to the wildlife and insect population. It seems the increase in environmental awareness has seen the spotlight move away from the more pristine cultivated planting that has dominated the world of gardening for so long and on to a new-found love of and appreciation for weeds/wildflowers.

DEFINING A WEED

In its most simplified form, a weed is a self-seeded plant growing somewhere that we humans don't want it to. One of the most recognisable examples of a garden weed is the dandelion (*Taraxacum officinale*). While it's a lawn-lover's nightmare, bees count on it as a first source of nectar in spring, a trait that many of us would associate with wildflowers. So why is it that a rogue dandelion on a pristine lawn or a buddleia bush growing between paving slabs isn't something we desire or enjoy?

From a gardener's point of view, a weed is often a thug that thrives so well in the unique habitat of the garden that it doesn't allow other more fragile plants in the space to grow. And it's these fragile plants that we have chosen ourselves.

But in different habitats, these weeds are sometimes plants we would seek out. A good example of this is thistles. They are particularly efficient colonisers and can be a real pain in a garden bed or new wildflower meadow, as they're likely to take over. Diversity is what a good gardener should be aiming for, and a garden full of thistles isn't that. But when managed and controlled, they are a plant that many of us enjoy. In floristry, they are a very popular cut flower and one that's often requested for weddings to add a wildflower look to the arrangements. They are also a plant that's valued for benefitting pollinators. You can see here how the lines are blurred when it comes to defining a weed or wildflower.

THE ENVIRONMENT AND NATURAL HABITATS

As gardeners, we must remember that we are guardians of nature. While we want to make the most beautiful environments for ourselves and those around us, we must also consider the micro-habitats we are creating. Our gardens should be a space for a diversity of plants, insects and animals alike. In recent years, there has been a rise in the popularity of the rewilding movement, where we aim to return ecosystems to their natural and uncultivated state where nature can take care of itself, restoring our relationship with the natural world in the process. Although this isn't something that's necessarily a priority for gardeners, whose principal aim is to create a place of beauty, it should be taken into consideration when designing and planting a healthy habitat.

One part of this is that we as a society have become increasingly aware of the detrimental effects that herbicides have on the natural world. Routine use of chemicals used to kill the plants we consider weeds threatens the lives of wild plants, birds, earthworms, hedgehogs, frogs and other animals. Not only are these chemicals used in domestic gardens, but in parks, pavements and even on roadsides. If a weed must be removed, it should always be done using sustainable practices, such as using water-permeable garden matting, through mulching and regular hoeing or, most commonly, by hand-weeding. While these methods may seem tedious or more difficult than using chemicals, it's helpful to keep in mind the joy we can get from simply being outdoors surrounded by nature. Using these techniques to keep weeds at bay is beneficial to the environment in the long run, and you might even find there are some 'weeds' you come to favour as wildflowers in the process.

WHAT WE CAN LEARN

There is a lot to learn from weeds and wildflowers, particularly for those of us who are just starting to garden or plant our own outdoor spaces. Anything that has self-sown is telling us that this particular environment is where they thrive and these are their favoured conditions. You'll likely find ferns growing on shaded, damp roadsides; hollyhocks (*Alcea*) thriving in the rubble on a parched building site; and yarrow (*Achillea*) running the lengths of motorways (highways). These are all examples of the right plant finding the right place, and we should try to learn from them and plant similar flowering plants in our outdoor spaces. For example, Alice has a hot and very bright south-facing balcony, and stonecrops (*Sedum*) and grasses have started to appear in many of her pots. This is an indication to try out some different grasses to add texture alongside the succulents she already knew thrived in that environment.

So, what is the difference between a weed and a wildflower? The bottom line is that some weeds are wildflowers and some wildflowers are weeds, and it all depends on your point of view and the current attitude towards weeds – right now, the best advice is to leave them be and let pollinators and local wildlife enjoy them.

Dandelions

Dandelions (*Taraxacum officinale*) belong to a genus of flowering perennial plants that boasts over 250 different species worldwide. The dandelion species is well known and beloved by children and wildflower-lovers alike, who relish blowing the parachuted seeds off its globular seedheads. In fact, such is the fascination with dandelions that the study of these plants even has its own name, taraxacology.

The botanical name of the dandelion provides insight into both the positive and negative connotations surrounding the plant. The genus name, Taraxacum, is thought to either come from the Arabic word *tarakhshagog*, which roughly translates to 'bitter herb', or the Greek word *tarasso*, which means 'to disturb'. The species name, officinale, is a denomination given to healing herbs, and means 'medicinal'.

The dandelion has been revered for its nutritional and healing properties throughout the ages, and its benefit to early pollinators and to the ecosystems in which they are found growing is invaluable.

Despite its positive associations, the plant's relentless determination to establish its presence in even the most meticulously kept gardens has led to its vilification as an invasive weed. Many who enjoy tending to ornamental gardens and lawns despair at the sight of the plant's distinctive rosette of leaves or sunshine-coloured flower when they appear out of place.

Ultimately, the debate lingers on – is the dandelion a weed, an unwanted intruder in our pristine landscapes? Or is it a wildflower, a sweet and charming symbol of resilience?

A BRIEF HISTORY OF THE DANDELION

Throughout recorded history, the dandelion has held a significant place as both a medicinal herb and a source of sustenance. The plant's origins stretch far back, with estimates suggesting that the genus has been around for at least 30 million years. Dandelions feature in ancient Egyptian, Roman, Arabic and Anglo-Saxon texts, and have been used in many cultures across the globe to treat a multitude of complaints.

Without understanding the nutritional science behind the herb, many ancient civilisations recognised it as a medicinal wonder. We now understand that a great number of ailments suffered before modern times were the result of vitamin-deficient diets – but why was the dandelion so good at curing these? It is because every part of the plant – the leaf, the root, the flower and the stem – is jam-packed with nutrients essential for keeping our bodies functional. Without access to these nutrients, disease and ill health are inevitable.

In fact, it has been found that a single dandelion plant contains more vitamin C than a tomato, and gram for gram it contains more vitamin A than spinach. It also contains copious amounts of iron, calcium, magnesium and potassium. This means that dandelions would have been extremely effective at warding off diseases such as scurvy, anaemia, rickets and other misunderstood ailments that plagued earlier civilisations.

Although the science doesn't go a long way to back it up, dandelions were also used in traditional medicine throughout the globe to treat liver disease, digestive issues, inflammation, fever, diarrhoea and countless other maladies. Although they have never been proven to cure any of the above, the nutrients and minerals the plant provides can only have helped to improve overall health while suffering from disease.

In fact, before this humble, nutritional plant was blacklisted as an invasive weed, people cultivated it as a food source. When other food was scarce, entire armies would use the plant to keep their strength up during battle, and dandelion salads feature in Greek mythological tales. The dandelion spread across the globe due to its nutritional benefits, and it has been passed from person to person and country to country throughout human history as a source of food and medicine.

The plant has also been used in other practical ways throughout history. Both the flowers and the leaves were used as dyes, with yellow dye being created from the flowers and purple from the leaves. Dandelions also contain liquid latex within their stems and leaves. This latex has similar properties to the latex found in the rubber tree (*Hevea brasiliensis*), which is the source of much of the world's natural rubber. The dandelion latex was historically harvested and used as a natural adhesive. Surprisingly, this usage was called upon again during the Second World War, when rubber was in extremely high demand and neither natural nor synthetic rubber could be produced quickly enough to supply all the armies fighting across the world. Building a single battleship used 75 tonnes (82 tons) of rubber, a tank needed 1 tonne (1½ tons) and military airplanes required 500 kg (1100 lb). Scientists looked to other sources for the material, and in the end Russian dandelions provided the answer.

Today, tinctures, teas and supplements made from dandelions are still used medicinally. They are used as diuretics, which allow the body to expel excess water and sodium through urine, as a digestive aid and to help detoxify the liver. Many people forage and eat young dandelion leaves, which have a similar taste to rocket (arugula) and are a wonderful addition to salads, omelettes, sandwiches and any other meal to which you might add leafy greens.

Besides human history, dandelions are also extremely beneficial to pollinators and other insects and animals. Because their flowers appear so early on in the year, they are essential to early awakening pollinators, who rely on any and all early flowers to survive. Northern hemisphere bees and fritillary butterflies use dandelions as a source of nectar during times when other flowers are still undeveloped. Certain birds, such as linnets, also rely on dandelions and dandelion seeds as a reliable food source throughout the year.

A NOXIOUS WEED

Despite the dandelion's varied uses, to many it is still considered a 'noxious weed' that is 'harmful to humans, livestock, agricultural or horticultural crops, natural habitats or ecosystems'. While this label may seem harsh, in some places, it isn't necessarily so far from the truth.

Dandelions, by nature, are incredibly invasive. Their lifecycle is short and once the flowers have appeared, the spherical head that follows – which is referred to by many as a 'clock' – carries thousands of seeds.

When they are ready, even the slightest hint of a breeze has the power to disperse each parachuted seed as far as 100 km (62 miles) from its starting point. This means that if you live in London, a dandelion in your lawn could have come all the way from Dover. Each dandelion that grows from each seed has the ability to produce thousands of seeds, which in turn produce thousands of dandelions, each with the ability to produce thousands of seeds – and so on. But if dandelions are so useful, what's the problem?

Since dandelions grow so quickly, they often end up overshadowing the seedlings of other species, stealing their nutrients, water and access to light. Attempts to remove them may also be difficult because of their long taproots. These taproots (not dissimilar to the roots of a carrot) are difficult to remove from the soil in a whole piece, and if any fragments remain in the earth, the plant will regrow quickly and without much difficulty. This makes things particularly tricky for those growing vegetables or any other seedlings outside. It also means that in well-manicured gardens, parks or sports fields, the appearance of a single dandelion can be extremely problematic. It's hard to imagine Lionel Messi scoring goals in a field full of lumpy-bumpy dandelions. Unfortunately, even far beyond the worlds of sports and gardening, dandelions have managed to wreak havoc on entire ecosystems.

Denali National Park in Alaska, USA, is a place of natural beauty, encompassing more than six million acres of land and preserving the habitat of thousands of species of plants, animals, fungi, mosses and insects – all of whom rely on a delicately balanced ecosystem for survival.

But the invasion of non-native plants poses a threat to the landscape. Without natural herbivores or diseases, these plants are free to devastate, outcompeting native plants and providing little benefit to the ecosystem. Dandelions aren't by any stretch the worst of these non-native plant species, but since they spread so far so easily and quickly, they do have the potential to be a serious threat.

Luckily, volunteers and rangers at Denali National Park have come up with an ingenious way of eradicating their most prolific problem plant: 'the Dandelion Demolition'. Each year, hundreds of volunteers of all ages gather in the national park, trowels in hand, to help rid the park of the species. In 2019, less than a hundred volunteers removed more than 130 kg (287 lb) of dandelions in just a few hours. This method of hand-removal is much more effective than strimming or removing en masse, since any roots leftover would simply sprout anew in a few days. Herbicides, which would be incredibly damaging to the ecosystem, are understandably out of the question.

While a few dandelions in the lawn are unlikely to cause many problems, the need for Denali's Dandelion Demolitions shows that even a plant with as many uses as the dandelion can still be a problematic presence in the wrong environmen.

WEED OR WILDFLOWER?

The *Oxford English Dictionary*'s definition of a weed is: 'A wild plant growing where it is not wanted and in competition with cultivated plants.' If we use this as our guide, then the ever-faithful dandelion certainly fits the description. But the presence of dandelions in the garden shouldn't be considered as something terrible – attempted eradication of the weed, especially if using weedkillers, may cause much more harm to the ecosystem than the plant does.

Perhaps, rather than feeling despair when we spy their distinctive leaves or bright petals in a man-made environment, we should instead learn to tolerate, even love, dandelions. Not just for their rich history and medicinal benefits, but for the tenacity and strength that sees them labelled as such a nuisance in the first place.

"Such plants are 'weeds' only to those who make a business of selling and applying chemicals."

—

Rachel Carson,
conservationist

Morning Glory and Bindweed

Native Locations

Morning Glory
Mesoamerica

Binweed
Europe and Asia

Morning glory is a complicated plant, because while this common name generally refers to an annual, twining vine cultivated for its beautiful flowers, it is sometimes used to refer to another plant known as bindweed, which is perhaps one of the most contentious weeds that modern gardeners battle with. To the untrained eye, both plants look incredibly similar, and that's because they belong to the same family, *Convolvulaceae*, and the family's characteristic trumpet-shaped flowers and twining habit of growth are present in both. While the names are often used interchangeably, each plant brings with it a different reaction from gardeners – bindweed is 'bad', while morning glory is 'good'.

Although they belong to the same family, bindweed belongs to the genus *Calystegia* or *Convolvulus*, while morning glory belongs to the genus *Ipomoea*, which is the largest genus in the family and also includes food crops such as sweet potatoes (*Ipomoea batatas*) and water spinach (*Ipomoea aquatica*). To avoid any confusion, we'll use 'morning glory' in reference to *Ipomoea*, and 'bindweed' in reference to *Calystegia* and *Convolvulus*.

MORNING GLORY

Of the two plants, morning glory is the one that is considered desirable, and new cultivars can be bought at garden centres and found in full bloom in horticultural displays, showing off their flowers in the sunshine. In fact, the reason the plant is called 'morning glory' is because its colourful flowers open up with the morning sun.

Although it isn't quite as tenacious as its undesirable counterpart, morning glory can still be quite invasive and its foliage can be challenging to control in a garden setting. Luckily, most cultivated varieties are annual plants, growing, flowering and setting seed before dying off, all within the same year. This means that with removal of the seeds, they aren't as difficult to keep at bay as other plants within their family. If the seeds are left on the plant and allowed to set in the soil for next year, however, this climbing vine can easily take over an entire garden. Avid horticulturalists therefore save the seeds and share them with friends and family so that they can also grow the vine.

Morning glory plants tend to have tuberous roots (potatoes are an example of a tuberous root). These roots are large and store starch to feed the plant. Because of this, a single plant is fairly easy to remove, and any roots leftover in the soil are likely to die before producing an overwhelming amount of new shoots.

Interestingly, morning glory plants operate in an 'each to their own' fashion, and species within the genus do little in the way of helping each other survive or thrive – in fact, they do the opposite. When growing in close proximity, members of the genus that belong to different species compete for pollinators, exuding more aroma and colour and even producing bigger flowers than their neighbours to win the affection of pollinators. This hinders the reproductive process of surrounding plants allowing them to reproduce and thrive in an environment untampered by their siblings. Still, many plant-lovers cultivate the fast-growing vine for its beautiful flowers, using it to cover trellises, pergolas, old sheds or structures with little visual value.

Another factor that contributes to the plant's desirability is its ease of cultivation. It thrives in an array of different soil types and requires very minimal care, it is resilient to many pests and diseases, and its hardiness and frost tolerance makes it adaptable to a variety of different climates, making it a popular choice in a range of geographical regions.

BINDWEED

To gardeners and horticulturalists, bindweed is synonymous with evil. The plant is infamous for its ability to spread with vigour, choking any other plant unfortunate enough to get in its way. But the word 'bindweed' is broad and can be used to describe many species within the *Convolvulaceae* family. The two main types of destructive bindweed are field bindweed (*Convolvulus arvensis*), which can be found growing mostly in open soils, barren sites and in wildflower meadows, and hedge bindweed (*Calystegia sepium*), which is more commonly found growing in cultivated land, like gardens or fields used for commercial agriculture.

Perhaps because of the differences in where the two are found growing, field bindweed is generally accepted as a wildflower, while hedge bindweed is commonly thought of as a weed. Although the two are extraordinarily similar, field bindweed is much less vigorous. But what is it that makes hedge bindweed so terrible? One of the main issues is that it grows so quickly. With a twining habit, the plant wraps itself around any surface, plant, shrub or sapling (young tree) like a boa constrictor, blocking out light and suffocating slow-growing plants with ease. Since the plant is perennial (meaning that it will live for more than two years), it cannot be relied on to disappear after a year's worth of havoc.

While bindweed is perennial, it's aerial (above ground) parts are tender and herbaceous. This means that during winter, when conditions are unfavourable, the plant dies back to its roots. However, this is where the real problem lies, as bindweed's true strength is underground.

Unlike morning glory, bindweed plants have rhizomatous roots. Rhizomes are root systems that function as underground stems, with the ability to spread and produce new plants from very small sections – mint is a classic example. In the case of bindweed, damaged rhizomes quickly produce new shoots, resulting in a multitude of new plants in a small area. The roots can penetrate to a depth of 5 metres (16½ feet) in the soil and can spread more than 2 metres (6½ feet) during the growing seasons of the year. This means that from early spring until late autumn (fall), the roots of a new bindweed plant can span a distance of 6 metres (20 feet) – and this doesn't even account for plants that are more than a year old.

Further to this, the roots are exceptionally brittle. Even the smallest fragment left in the ground by a spade or hand will regrow as easily as if it were a whole network of roots, creating more and more new plants to contend with, much like the serpentine monster of Greek myth, the hydra, which sprouted two new heads as soon as any of its original nine were cut off.

When bindweed appears in a garden, it is almost impossible to fully eradicate. While many gardeners and agriculturalists may attempt to compete with the plant using physical control methods, such as smothering the plants so they die without light or hand-removal, most efforts are made in vain, since the roots live on. Unfortunately, the quickest and most effective approach to removing established bindweed involves using harmful and toxic herbicides, such as glyphosate, which kills any and all parts of a plant it comes into contact with. These kinds of toxic herbicides have been proven to cause extensive damage, not only to plants, but also to humans, animals, wildlife, fungi and aquatic life in the area in which they are used.

WILDLIFE WARRIORS

While morning glory and bindweed both have their demerits, they can also be invaluable to the ecosystem around them when growing in the wild.

As well as being coveted by horticulturalists, morning glory is also highly desired by a multitude of species, both insect and bird. This is often overlooked by those who cultivate the plant, since most are more interested in its visual appeal. All parts of the plant are useful to wildlife. The foliage provides food for many species of caterpillar and other herbivorous insects, the seeds are a favourite of songbirds and quails (this is also beneficial to gardeners who aren't looking to grow the plant continually) and the nectar in its flowers provide a stable source of food for many insects and birds.

Because the plant is so widely distributed, it plays an important role in different ecosystems across the globe. The ruby-throated hummingbird, which is prolific in North America in the summer and Central America in winter, is particularly fond of morning glory nectar, and can often be found feeding from its flowers. Likewise, the clouded skipper butterfly, also native to North and Central America as well as South America, adores the flowers and is a regular visitor to anywhere that cultivates the plant. Many other species of butterfly, moth and bee also frequent the flower, enjoying the nectar and pollinating the plant along the way.

The real unsung hero, however, is the more contentious of the two plants: bindweed. Although notoriously miserable to deal with in cultivated land, field bindweed is invaluable to insects and animals in the places it is found growing wild – and since it grows so quickly and easily, it is available in abundance to those who feed from it. It is essential to the survival of many species of bee and butterfly in wildflower meadows.

The foliage of field bindweed also provides food for over 80 species of herbivorous insect. Without this plant in the wild, all of these species would be without one of their most easily accessible, fast-growing food sources, and would have to find their dinner elsewhere to survive. This means that other plants that grow with less vigour in the places where field bindweed grows would be eaten instead – and this would have a knock-on effect on the entire ecosystem.

Further to this, field bindweed plays host to a species of moth so reliant on the genus that it has taken its name from the plant's family – the convolvulus hawk-moth. Without field bindweed providing foliage for the young caterpillars, the adult moth population would drop. The adult moths, who have long proboscises, play a vital role in pollinating plants like petunias, lilies and phlox, which have long nectar-baring spurs. Insects with smaller proboscises are unable to feed from the flowers and so do not complete the pollination cycle. Without hawk-moths, these flowers would have a much harder time finding worthy pollinators and their numbers would drop as a result.

These examples are just a few of many that we could use to illustrate the vital role that 'undesirable' species play in the ecosystems they thrive in, and how their eradication could have a catastrophic effect on the wildlife surrounding their natural habitats. Sometimes the plants that are so contentious to us in our cultivated lands are vital to the lives of the animals and insects we love to observe in our gardens.

"What would the world be, once bereft
Of wet and of wildness?
Let them be left,
O let them be left,
wildness and wet;
Long live the weeds
and the wilderness yet."

—

Gerard Manley Hopkins,
poet

CHAPTER 4

POLLINATION

Passion Flowers

Native Locations
Mexico, Central
America, the United
States and South
America

Pollination is an interesting and diverse topic due to the diversity of success among every flowering species, but it becomes even more fascinating when the subject under observation is a unique plant like the passion flower (*Passiflora*). There are few flowers with such otherworldly qualities, and as such they have the ability to captivate the average admirer and plant experts alike. It is almost unbelievable that they can survive as easily in the UK as they can in Italy, India or Australia.

FLORAL STRUCTURE

There are many different species of passion flower, and each has a different colour, size and coronal filament shape, but they all have complex flower heads that are symmetrical, colourful and extraordinarily attractive. And, although there are deviations from the norm, most passion flower species have similar and distinctive floral structures. To explore this further, we'll use the blue passion flower (*Passiflora caerulea*), one of the more common and widely grown species, as a structural example.

Starting from the exterior, the flower has five petals and five sepals, which alternate around the perimeter of the flower. Since the flower is nyctinastic (opens during the day and closes at night), the sepals facilitate the closing of the flower by pushing against the petals and gently closing the flower and its reproductive parts to preserve pollen during the night. The sepals can often be distinguished from the petals of a passion flower due to their pointed or tendrilled tips. When the flower closes at night, they are visible to us as the outside of the bud.

Next, almost floating atop the petals and sepals, are the corona filaments. Differing from filaments that hold up anthers and their pollen, these form a ring of long, thin 'petals' around the centre of the flower, which stretch out towards the tip. In some species of passion flower these corona filaments are curled and extend way beyond the perimeter of the petals, while in others they are totally straight and fall short of the edge of the flower. Some are white, some are red, many are purple and white, almost all are multicoloured, and all of them are symmetrical. In *P. caerulea*, the filaments are straight and relatively short, with a burgundy centre, a white middle and lilac tips. One main purpose of the corona filaments is to guide insects, birds and other pollinators towards the reproductive parts of the flower. This is perhaps why these are the most beguiling and diverse feature across different species and varieties of passion flower.

In the centre of the flower, a long, pillar-like stalk known as an androgynophore can be found. Surrounding the base of the androgynophore are more filaments, known as the operculum. This mass of dense, thin, vertical filaments creates a delicate barrier between the androgynophore and the nectaries.

Despite the variety found in other parts of the passion flower, the reproductive structures of most species of the plant are the same, with the androgynophore holding up five anthers, the ovary above these and three stigmas above the ovary. The five anthers typically hang upside down facing the flower, perhaps an inch or even two from the surface, and the female stigmas are either suspended just above these, or, in some species, sit atop erect styles connected to the ovary.

Although the reproductive parts of the passion flower are in such close proximity to one another, most passion flowers are self-incompatible. This means that even if the pollen from the anthers reaches the sticky stigma, the ovary will not produce viable fruit and the seeds will be sterile. The flowers therefore rely on pollinators to produce seed, and so they have come up with ways to make sure that insects and birds that visit the flower help them to pollinate and don't simply steal the nectar reward. Passion flowers may be flamboyant – but they must also be taken seriously.

PICKING A POLLINATOR

As a genus, *Passiflora* boasts some 550 species, and is perhaps the biggest show-off in the world of angiosperms (flowering plants). The living creatures that the plants are trying to impress are their pollinators, and they achieve this extremely well, with each flower perfectly paired to its own pollinator.

The genus as a whole is pollinated by myriad winged animals and insects, and the pairing of specific species with pollinator is mostly dependent on where the plant grows and which pollinator is most prevalent there. These pollinators include many types of bees, moths, butterflies, bats, hummingbirds and occasionally wasps.

In Australia, most passion flowers are pollinated by honey or carpenter bees (the latter being preferable due to their greater size). In the UK, bees are also the flower's main pollinator, with the notorious fuzzy-backed bumblebees taking over from their Australian carpenter counterparts. In the Andes, the sword-billed hummingbird is the main pollinator for one species of passion flower, *Passiflora mixta*, the long, nectar-bearing spurs of which are a perfect fit for the long bill of the hummingbird. In Ecuador, *Passiflora unipetala* is pollinated by bats, which, far from being shy, stick their entire heads into the tunnel-like flower to drink the nectar, covering the backs of their necks in pollen in the process.

These pollinator-flower couples are extremely successful and benefit both parties equally. The flowers are pollinated by the insects, bats and birds, and in turn the animals are rewarded with sweet, energy-rich nectar. But with the anthers suspended so high above the nectaries, the flower must be sure that the pollinators who visit it are large enough to brush past the pollen before collecting their nectar reward.

As much as the colourful filaments and other floral components are made to entice worthy pollinators, they are also carefully considered structural hurdles, designed to make life complicated for smaller insects and chancers. With such a jumble of filaments, fibres and stalks to climb, only the worthy make it to the nectaries. Of course, for a large insect such as the carpenter bee or bumblebee, these obstructions are no challenge at all – but for a smaller insect like a fly or small moth, the filaments and other fiddly bits are difficult obstacles for their small, delicate limbs. The struggle and loss of energy is hardly worth the nectar at the end.

Even if the smaller insects manage the exhausting hike through the filaments, the mass of dense, thin fibres that constitute the operculum create a delicate barrier that only the longest of beaks or proboscises could penetrate. These obstructions mean that those that wish to reach the nectar must be large enough to brush past the anther and carry the sticky, heavy pollen. This is an exchange, not a free-for-all.

NECTAR ROBBERS

Some devious insects recognise that the work isn't worth the reward, and have figured out crafty shortcuts to get to a plant's nectar – after all, why waste time on this floral obstacle course when you can have your fill without exhausting yourself in the process?

Known in the scientific community as 'nectar robbers', these insects (and sometimes birds) bypass the pollination exchange by drilling or biting holes in the base of the flower in order to reap the nectar rewards from the outside. Unfortunately, this often renders the flower useless. The passion plant has wasted precious energy producing such a complex flower, but, without achieving pollination, has nothing to show for it.

Once the holes have been made by one insect, all the other insects that visit the flower are able to easily access the nectar without completing the obstacle course, and their part in the nectar theft makes them 'secondary robbers'. Many species that would be unable to drink from the flower in the first place, including ants, butterflies, flies and wasps, can now feed from the flower for free. If the flower's nectar stores are heavily depleted, legitimate pollinators will choose to bypass the flower in favour of a better floral reward.

Many different species of insect and animal can undertake nectar robbery, but luckily it doesn't always mean the demise of the flower or plant. Bumblebees, for example, are one of the more well-documented primary nectar robbers, but since they also rely on the collection of pollen to feed their young, they usually end up pollinating the flower anyway.

Sunflowers

Native Location
North America

Sunflowers (*Helianthus annuus*) are perhaps one of the most recognisable flowers to have ever graced the globe. As children, they may be the first flower we become familiar with, and they have been immortalised in works of art and in myth and legend. With their striking yellow petals and dark centres, sunflowers never fail to catch the attention of floral enthusiasts everywhere. The flower itself holds myriad different meanings across different cultures and countries: it represents adoration, loyalty and longevity, and many associate its image with happiness.

Both the plant's common and botanical names make clear reference to the sun. Helianthus, the plant's Latin genus name, is derived from the Greek *helios*, meaning 'sun'. In Greek myth, Helios was the god of, and by many accounts the personification of, the sun. Therefore, all words beginning with 'helio' directly relate to the sun. Heliotropism, for example, which we will take a look at a little later on, is used to describe the tendency of a plant or flower to follow the sun – a well-known characteristic of sunflowers.

MORE THAN MEETS THE EYE

Sunflowers may seem like they have relatively straightforward flowers, but they are actually quite complex. What we perceive as being a single flower head is what's known in the botanical world as an 'inflorescence'. This is a single flower head comprised of many flowers – and in the case of sunflowers, many hundreds of them. From a distance, we see petals circling the outer perimeter of a flower with a dark, almost black centre. But if we venture slightly closer, an entirely new composition becomes apparent.

The bright yellow outer petals are known as 'ray florets', each of which is its own sterile flower. These florets serve the simple function of attracting pollinators to the real flowers by standing out as the most beguiling and colourful part of the flower head. But, since they are sterile and contain no nectar, the pollinating insect must explore further to obtain its reward.

The deep burgundy centre of the flower may seem as though it hasn't got much to offer, and perhaps to the uninterested eye of a simple human, this is true – but to a pollinating insect with heightened senses, this is where the real prize lies. The centre of the inflorescence is occupied by hundreds and sometimes thousands of tiny, fertile flowers, each prepared to offer a nectar reward to any insect willing to pollinate them. These miniscule flowers, each measuring no more than 5 mm (¼ inch), are known as 'disc florets'.

Each individual disc floret is hermaphroditic (both male and female). A mature flower will first push up its male flower part, which protrudes past the low edges of the petals, so that pollinators must come into contact with pollen if they want to claim their nectar. After this, the disc floret's female flower part takes over, and the sticky stigma has the chance to receive the pollen and complete the pollination cycle.

BULLSEYE

Many pollinating insects are able to see wavelengths of light that are imperceptible to the naked human eye. Because of this, some species of flowers have created incredible displays that can only be perceived by human eyes with the aid of ultra-violet lightbulbs, but which are visible and very attractive under normal conditions to insects such as bees. Flowers use these displays to highlight and guide pollinators to the sexual parts of the flower to achieve successful pollination. The better the display, the greater the chance of success.

Since the disc florets of a sunflower are so miniscule, with little to no attracting qualities, they could easily be overlooked by pollinators, and so the sunflower has to find another way to attract its pollinating friends to the tiny, fertile flowers. Under UV light, the plant's flower heads display a gigantic bullseye. This directs pollinators straight into the centre of the flower, where the small disc florets are located.

Interestingly, scientists from the University of British Columbia who studied this pollinator-attracting feature made another fascinating discovery. Sunflowers growing in hotter climates seemed to have bigger bullseyes, while those growing in more temperate climates had smaller bullseyes. But since both would benefit greatly from the former, why don't both bullseyes grow to the same size, regardless of climate? It seems that the attractive feature created by the flower isn't only there for the benefit of pollinators.

The researchers found that a single gene, called HaMYB111, was responsible for the bullseye pattern created by species in the sunflower genus. This gene has also been found to help plants survive under a wide range of environmental stressors, such as drought, extremes in temperature and low humidity levels. Plants that live in these high-stress environments are more likely to produce more of the gene in order to survive, so in turn, the flowers produce bigger bulls-eyes. This effectively kills two birds with one stone, and it is an amazing example of how plants and flowers are able to overcome multiple obstacles with a single adaptation.

FOLLOWING THE SUN

As we briefly touched on earlier, heliotropism is a characteristic many plants and flowers display in which they turn or change the way they are growing in order to face or follow the sun. In fact, the word heliotropism literally translates to 'sun turn'. Most of us are familiar with the distinctive way that sunflowers turn their flower heads to face the rays of sunshine.

However, research from the University of California, Davis suggests that mature sunflowers are not heliotropic at all, and instead indicates that only sunflowers in their juvenile stage of growth display these movements. The reason juvenile sunflowers display this behaviour concerns the plant's circadian rhythm. Circadian rhythms in plants function in much the same ways as they do for humans, insects and animals, and can be best described as changes in behaviour or physiology based on the 24-hour clock. This pattern is also referred to as the sleep/wake cycle, and is usually a response to the light of day and the darkness of night.

As it turns out, young sunflower plants respond to this circadian rhythm very differently to their mature counterparts. The reason they seem to follow the sun is because opposite sides of their stems elongate during different times in the 24-hour cycle. At night, the western side of the stem elongates, pushing the budding flower head to face east, while during the day, the eastern side of the stem elongates in response to the sun, pushing the flower head to the west. That means that if we track a juvenile sunflower through the day, its flower seems to track the sun, moving from east to west.

As the sunflower matures, however, growth slows down, and once it reaches full maturity, it stops. The face of the sunflower then always faces east to greet the rising sun in the morning. The reason they do this is also for the benefit of pollinators, since bees and other flying insects rise early and would prefer to feed from a sun-warmed flower – so sunflowers face east to accommodate their flying friends.

"Being able to coordinate in this way makes them a better target for bees… It's a strategy to attract as many insects as possible."

—

Stacey Harmer,
chronobiologist & professor
of biology at the University
of California, Davis

Hydrangeas

Native Locations
America and Asia

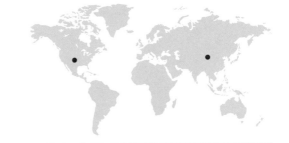

Hydrangeas, most well known for their large, showy flowers, have become more and more popular over the years. From bouquets and gardens to floral displays, there aren't many flowers that have the same impact as the cloud-like hydrangea.

Belonging to a small family of plants, *Hydrangeaceae*, which is named after the genus, *Hydrangea*, there are around 75 species of hydrangea native to Japan, China, Korea and other East Asian countries, encompassing a wide variety of different shapes, sizes, colours and levels of hardiness. But beyond their basic attributes, hydrangeas hold a few subtle secrets and shapeshifting qualities that make the plant and its flowers more intriguing than they might initially appear.

THE BRACT OF THE MATTER

There are many different species of hydrangea, each with their own distinctively shaped flower head, and the plants are unofficially categorised by their leaf shapes, flower shapes and their habit of growth. They can be referred to as mophead hydrangeas, lacecaps, flatheads, mountain hydrangeas, bigleaf hydrangeas, oakleaf hydrangeas and climbing hydrangeas – among many other names.

Perhaps the most common and widely grown species is *Hydrangea macrophylla*, also known as the 'bigleaf hydrangea', so to avoid any confusion, we'll use this as our example.

When we think of hydrangeas, the image that comes to mind is usually of one big, cloud-like flowering head. But, much like sunflowers (page 78), hydrangea flower heads are actually inflorescences. This means that what we perceive as a single large flower head is actually a collection of many small flowers clustered together.

Each individual floret contains two types of flower. The first, and most visible, is the sterile outer flower, which is comprised of sepals rather than petals. Sepals are a type of modified leaf that usually form on the outside of flowers to offer protection while the flower is in bud. In the case of hydrangeas, they serve as the pollinator-attracting petals, providing a showy display that shouts, 'We have nectar! Come and pollinate us!'

Nestled deep within the centre of the hard-working sepal is a miniscule second flower. Measuring no more than 1 cm (½ inch) in width, this flower holds the real power. Containing both the male and female flower parts that are necessary for reproduction, it is essential for the continuation of the species. Although this fertile flower is arguably the most important of the two, one without the other would not be able to survive, so both flowers work in tandem to achieve successful pollination.

Hydrangeas are not the only flowers that manage to attract pollinators without showy flowers to back them up, though – there are a multitude of plants that use modified leaves as a way to attract pollinators to small, unscented flowers. Although hydrangeas use sepals for this purpose, many other plants use another type of modified leaf known as a bract to make themselves more visible. A few notable examples are clematis, bougainvillea, anthurium, poinsettias and crocuses. All of these plants use brightly coloured, showy bracts to draw in pollinators and achieve successful pollination. Sometimes the bracts surrounding the flower are masterful in their ability to keep up with real flowers – some have even been known to emit scent.

While the bracts' main goal is to fit in with the flowers unnoticed, there is one distinguishable feature that tells them apart – veins. Much like a true leaf, these modified leaves still contain venation, albeit more spaced out, whereas their petal counterparts do not.

Overall, these bracts and sepals go a long way to ensure the survival of plants with small flowers. By leveraging the plant's visual appeal, bracts effectively communicate to pollinators that a rewarding nectar or pollen source awaits them, compelling them to investigate further and engage in the essential act of pollination.

SHOWING THEIR COLOURS

One of the most intriguing characteristics of *Hydrangea macrophylla* is its ability to change colour depending on the acidity or alkalinity of its soil. This fascinating phenomenon is unique to hydrangeas and has captivated the curiosity of gardeners and nature enthusiasts alike.

While the ability to change colour may seem like a magic trick, the science behind it is quite simple, and can be attributed to the presence of aluminium ions in the soil. In acidic soil, aluminium is more easily dissolved in water and therefore becomes available for uptake by the roots. Anthocyanin, the pigment responsible for the blue colour found in nature, relies on aluminium ions to bond and become active in hydrangea plants – so when the plant is able to absorb these ions, the flowers turn blue. Conversely, in alkaline soil, aluminium becomes less accessible, and the anthocyanin molecules cannot stick together, giving the flowers a pink or even red appearance. In more neutral soils, the flowers either become a mix of blue and pink or take on the colour made from that mix: purple.

Interestingly, studies have shown that the dynamic between hydrangeas and their pollinators also changes depending on the colour of the blooms. Some pollinators, like bees and butterflies, show preferences for particular colours. In the case of hydrangeas, the variation in colour can influence the type and number of pollinators that visit the plant. Bees are naturally more attracted to blue and purple flowers, while butterflies tend to prefer warmer and brighter colours, such as red and pink. This means that a hydrangea growing in acidic soil, with a blue or purple bloom, is likely to attract a high number of bees, while a hydrangea growing in alkaline soil, with pink or red flowers, is likely to attract a higher number of butterflies.

This remarkable colour-changing characteristic, beyond its aesthetic appeal, influences pollination and captures human interest, adding a touch of wonder to the world of flowers. Not only this, but it serves as a reminder of the intricate relationships between plants and their environment.

"Interconnectedness
is a fundamental
principle of nature.
Nothing is isolated.
Each event connects
with others."

—

Jon Kabat-Zinn,
professor

CHAPTER 5

POISONOUS
FLOWERS

Monkshood

Native Location
Central and
Western Europe

Perhaps the most notorious poisonous plant, monkshood or wolfsbane (*Aconitum*) has been widely used both medicinally and as a method of poisoning since the plant was discovered (before 90 AD by some accounts). Its beautiful, decorative flowers are shaped like hoods or helmets (hence the common name 'monkshood') and are clustered together in racemes, which means that each flower sits at the end of a thin stalk peppering a long, tall stem. The flowers are most commonly deep blue or purple, but can also be white, yellow, pink or pale green.

The other common name for monkshood, wolfsbane, comes from its use by the ancient Greeks, who tipped arrows with the plant in order to poison wolf packs, and also used it to tip javelins and swords used in battle to kill their enemies. The Anglo-Saxons similarly used monkshood to poison bait meant for wolves and other predatory animals. In Northern Europe, it is said that the berserkers, famous warriors who worshipped the Norse god Odin, ate monkshood in order to transform themselves in to fearsome werewolves.

The plant and its flowers have been immortalised through history and in many fictional stories. In the famous book and film series *Harry Potter*, wolfsbane is used in a potion by Professor Lupin to control his werewolf ability. In Greek myth, the plant is used regularly as a source of transformation – in Ovid's *Metamorphoses*,

for example, monkshood is used by Athena to turn Arachne into a spider after she humiliates the goddess with her superior weaving skills. According to another Greek legend, monkshood is the product of the toxic dribble produced by the gigantic and hideous hell-hound, Cerberus, who was captured by Hercules for his twelfth labour.

MODE OF POISONING

So, what is it that makes monkshood so toxic? As with many plants, the deadly nature of the *Aconitum* genus is the result of a complex make-up of different chemicals, and in particular, the toxic alkaloid named after the plant, aconitine. This toxin is also present in other members of the *Ranunculaceae* family (the family that *Aconitum* belongs to) like delphiniums, which are also poisonous, though to a much lesser degree.

Alkaloids are a type of naturally occurring organic compound (like proteins, carbohydrates, DNA, sugars, etc.) that can be produced by almost any living thing, and although alkaloids are most commonly found in plants and fungi, they can occasionally be observed in animals and bacteria as well. Two well-known examples of alkaloids are morphine and codeine (both of which are derived from plants). Other familiar alkaloids include those that are stimulating and have effects on our central nervous system – such as caffeine (found in cocoa, tea and coffee plants) and nicotine (derived from plants in the nightshade family) – and those that are psychotropic – such as psilocin, which together with psilocybin creates the psychedelic reaction associated with the ingestion of magic mushrooms.

The alkaloids found in monkshood are both highly powerful cardiotoxins (toxins affecting the heart) and neurotoxins (toxins affecting the nervous system), and they in exist in all parts of the plant in high concentration. Alongside aconitine, alkaloids such as jesaconitine, mesaconitine, hypaconitine and many others come together to create a truly noxious concoction. This means that ingesting even a small amount (as little as 1 g) of the plant can be fatal.

If someone were to ingest monkshood, the effects on the body would be disastrous, and without medical intervention would almost always result in a horrific death. The symptoms begin in the peripheral nervous system; the first sign of poisoning, felt anywhere between two minutes and two hours after ingestion, is a faint tingling, starting at the extremities and slowly taking over the entire body. After that, the poison begins to affect the gastrointestinal system, with symptoms such as stomach cramps, abdominal pain and nausea leading swiftly on to severe vomiting and diarrhoea. Once these symptoms have appeared, casualties have been known to experience headaches, sweating, salivation, an irregular heartbeat, dizziness, bodily numbness, loss of vision, chest pain, shortness of breath and other unpleasant symptoms. Eventually, the person will no longer be able to move due to muscular paralysis and their kidneys and liver will likely begin to shut down, after which there are two fatal outcomes: they either succumb to respiratory paralysis (the inability to breathe) or cardiac arrest (heart failure).

It is not only those who eat the plant who suffer from symptoms, though. Aconitine can easily be absorbed through the skin, so gardeners, florists and foragers who handle the plant carelessly may also notice its effects. Numbness and tingling are often felt at the site where skin comes into contact with the plant, followed by increased salivation and headaches. These symptoms rarely amount to anything life-threatening, but on occasion can cause cardiac arrythmia (irregular heartbeat) – enough to warrant careful handling of the plant.

Unfortunately, there is no known antidote for monkshood poisoning. The only medical intervention available is the management of symptoms. Hospitals can give casualties medicine to regulate their heart rate (ironically, hospitals may use medicine derived from another poisonous plant, deadly nightshade, to increase the heart rate of the patient), they can provide oxygen for those struggling to breathe, and they can provide fluids through an IV to maintain hydration during the ordeal. Thankfully, if hospitalised immediately, most patients will survive the poisoning.

MONKSHOOD POISONINGS
THROUGH HISTORY

Most instances of monkshood poisoning, both accidental and homicidal, occurred before the modern day, not least since poisoning is no longer a common homicidal tactic due to advancements in science and detection. Almost all types of poison are now traceable and because of this, most modern instances of monkshood poisoning are the result of improperly concocted herbal remedies, or food preparation gone wrong.

However, earlier in history, death by monkshood poisoning was relatively common, and the plant was used in murderous acts and as punishment imposed on prisoners by judicial systems (this was particularly popular in ancient Greece). Extraordinarily, the two most recent instances of murder using this poison in the UK are separated by more than 100 years.

The murder of Lakhvinder Cheema

The most recent instance of monkshood poisoning in the UK was in 2009, when a west London-based woman named Lakhvir Singh murdered her lover of 16 years. The victim, Lakhvinder Cheema, broke off his relationship with Singh to pursue an engagement to another woman. On hearing the news, Singh became enraged. She urged Cheema to break off his relationship, but he refused and the new couple began planning their wedding. Cheema's fiancée urged Singh to leave them in peace on several occasions, but was always met with confrontation, refusal and hostility.

Singh, now conscious of the fast-approaching wedding date, booked a flight to India to purchase *bikh*, a poison made from *Aconitum ferox* that is used in traditional Indian medicine to treat fevers and inflammatory conditions. When she returned to the UK, she visited Cheema's home and poisoned a curry she found in the refrigerator that she knew the couple would eat while going over wedding plans later that evening.

Sure enough, when Cheema returned to home that evening, he and his fiancée warmed the curry to eat for dinner. Cheema had second helpings of the dish, and soon after he finished his meal, he began to complain of sickness and stomach cramps. Not long after, he started to vomit violently. His fiancée reported that Cheema said his entire body had gone numb. He then lost the ability to move or see properly. Soon afterwards, Cheema's fiancée started to feel similar symptoms, reporting a stomach ache, dizziness and difficulty standing on her own. Cheema dialled 999 and requested an ambulance, telling the operator that he thought their food had been poisoned by his ex-girlfriend.

While waiting for the ambulance, the couple's condition declined even further, so Cheema called his sister, who rushed them to hospital. Within an hour of arrival, Lakhvinder Cheema was pronounced dead. His fiancée was placed into a medically induced coma for two days while her symptoms were monitored and treatment administered, and she made a full recovery.

The doctors identified the poison and when Singh was arrested and searched, they found traces of the same poison in the pocket of her coat. Singh was found guilty and sentenced to 36 years in prison for the murder of her former lover and the attempted murder of his new fiancée.

The murder of Percy Malcolm John

George Henry Lamson was a US-born decorated doctor and volunteer surgeon based in the UK. His record was impeccable, and he had been awarded several medals and awards while serving overseas, including the Legion of Honour in France. In 1878, Lamson moved to Bournemouth, on the south coast of England, and married Kate John, one of five orphaned siblings. Her parents and one of her three sisters had died before the couple were wed, and each of the remaining siblings – two brothers and two sisters – had inherited the wealth of the deceased.

During this time in British history, married women were not afforded their own wealth or inheritance. Instead, any money, property or valuable items that the woman inherited were automatically passed into the hands of their husbands. That meant that upon their marriage, Lamson inherited the wealth his wife had received following the death of her parents and sister.

In 1879, shortly after their marriage, another of Kate's brothers, Herbert John, passed away, leaving £700 ($875) to Lamson. He used this money to open a surgery in Bournemouth, all the while living a life of luxury that he could not have afforded on his own, and supporting a serious addiction to morphine, which he had acquired during his service. This taste for the finer things in life, addiction and the subsequent deterioration of his surgery meant that Lamson ended up in considerable amounts of debt. He was refused any loans he attempted to take out and his financial situation was in a state of ruin.

Kate's remaining brother, 19-year-old Percy Malcolm John, used a wheelchair due to partial paralysis and attended a boarding school in Wimbledon, London. He was due to inherit £3,000 ($3,750) on his 21st birthday, but if he died before then, the money would be split between Lamson and the husband of Kate's one living sister.

In desperation, Lamson travelled from Bournemouth to London to pawn items and attempt to borrow money. Before his visit to London, however, he sent a letter to Percy telling him that he was due to visit his father in Italy but would drop by and say farewell before he left.

On 3 December 1881, Lamson had tea with Percy and his schoolmaster, Mr Bedbrook. He had brought with him a pre-cut fruitcake, which the three ate with their tea. Lamson told Mr Bedbrook that he'd been abroad and had discovered a new way to administer medicine to the boys at the school, producing an empty capsule for the schoolmaster to look at. He then suggested that Percy take a pill to show his schoolmaster how easy they were to swallow. Spooning some sugar into a seemingly empty capsule, he handed the pill over to Percy, who took it without question.

Almost immediately, Lamson took out his watch and told the pair that he must leave or he'd be late to catch his train. Mr Bedbrook accompanied Lamson to the door, where Lamson remarked that he didn't think Percy had much time left to live – supposedly because of his paralysis, although this seemed strange, as Percy was otherwise in perfectly good health.

Before half an hour had passed, Percy began to complain to his schoolmaster of heartburn. He said he felt the same way he had when Lamson had given him a pill on a previous occasion. Soon after this, Percy became seriously unwell – he began vomiting and was taken up to his bedroom to rest. He continued to vomit violently, eventually having to be held down by his schoolmaster and two doctors as he was writhing in such agony. Realising there was nothing they could do to save the boy, the doctors administered morphine to ease his pain. Percy fell into a coma and died less than four hours after swallowing the pill Lamson had given him.

A sample of vomit was taken to be examined and monkshood poisoning was found to be the cause of death. It was found that the cake Lamson had given Percy and the capsule he'd swallowed had both contained enough poison to kill the boy. Lamson, who believed the poison would be untraceable, was arrested and tried at the Old Bailey, where he was found guilty of murdering his brother-in-law to obtain his inheritance. On 28 March 1881, at the age of 30, George Henry Lamson was hanged for his crime.

Foxgloves

Flowers are often associated with beauty, fragrance and joy, but not all blooms have such a positive reputation. Foxgloves (*Digitalis*) are well known for their handsome flowers, their place in fairy tale and myth (page 16), their medicinal properties and also their toxicity. The plant and its derivative chemicals have been used for centuries to treat heart conditions and an array of other medical ailments, but the same chemicals that are used for good are also notorious for causing serious harm when the plant is ingested raw.

MODE OF POISONING

Poisons in plants come in the form of naturally occurring organic compounds. In monkshood (page 92), these are toxic alkaloids, but in foxgloves, the main compounds that are responsible for the plant's toxicity are known as cardiac glycosides. As their name suggests, cardiac glycosides primarily affect the function of the heart, and those who ingest the poison may experience either tachycardia (a faster than normal heart rate) or bradycardia (a slower than normal heart rate) as a baseline symptom.

Plants that contain cardiac glycosides have been used throughout history and across the globe as a medicine, as well as in rat

poisons, to tip poison arrows or as a homicidal or suicidal aid. Due to advancements in science, however, cardiac glycosides are now mostly used in properly tested doses within the field of medicine.

While this type of compound is present in many different species of plant, it is perhaps most well documented in foxgloves, which have been poisoning humans and animals for over four centuries. In fact, foxglove poisoning is so well documented that it even has its own name – digitalism. Poisoning can either be acute or chronic and can cause an array of unpleasant symptoms. While the most prominent and deadly effect is on the heart, many other parts of the body are affected too, and the poisoned person (or animal) is likely to suffer a great deal before either being treated, or, if the dose is high enough, succumbing to the poison.

The initial symptoms of poisoning begin between three and six hours after ingestion of the toxin, and then progress rapidly. The toxins affect almost all parts of the body and can be fatal very quickly in high doses. They vary from person to person, and not all symptoms will be present in every individual.

The victim will suffer from various mental and visual disturbances, including confusion, dizziness, pinpointed or dilated pupils, vertigo, fatigue, drowsiness, blurred vision and headaches. They may experience gastrointestinal problems, including stomach cramps, nausea, vomiting and bloody diarrhoea. The central nervous system and heart also suffer – symptoms such as muscle weakness, tremors, palpitations and convulsions are common, alongside an irregular heartbeat. If left long enough without treatment, the casualty will die.

In some cases of prolonged poisoning, such as with Dutch artist Vincent Van Gogh (page 104), foxgloves can cause depression, and the poisoned individual may observe yellow halos around objects in their line of vision.

FOXGLOVE: FRIEND OR FOE?

While the infamous foxglove may seem like a devilish flower, it isn't all bad. As with most things, the dose makes the poison, and cardiac glycosides derived from foxglove plants can be extremely beneficial in regulated quantities. The drug digoxin, which is derived from foxgloves, is one of the oldest medications used in cardiology – physicians, herbalists and cardiologists have been using the plant and its extracts to treat an array of health problems for centuries.

The juice from the crushed leaves of the foxglove is said to have been used as early as the 13th century as a topical medicine in Wales and Italy. Physicians during this period used this foliar extract to treat boils, sores, swelling and scabbing. A little later on, in 1785, British physician William Withering wrote a book called *An Account of the Foxglove and some of its Medical Uses*, in which he listed various medicinal properties of the plant. He claimed it could be used to treat epilepsy, oedema, hydrothorax and tuberculosis, among an array of other sicknesses, and foxgloves were used to treat these ailments long after the book was published.

Today, digoxin is widely used to treat a number of cardiovascular health problems. Since cardiac glycosides help to strengthen and slow the heart rate, the drug is often used in cases of arrythmia (irregular heartbeat) and heart failure. However, digoxin is still administered with extreme care due to its narrow 'therapeutic index'. The therapeutic index of a medicine is the window in which a drug is safe for a patient. A minor overdose of a drug with a narrow therapeutic index, such as digoxin (or morphine, for example) could be fatal, whereas an overdose of a drug with a very wide therapeutic index (like valerian root or cannabis) would cause no lasting harm to the patient. Further to this, even when taken in the recommended doses, nausea, diarrhoea and dizziness are still common side effects of digoxin. And, if a patient is prescribed digoxin, they may eventually suffer from a build-up in the system, known as 'digoxin toxicity', at which point the symptoms become scarily similar to those of foxglove ingestion. In order to counteract this, scientists have created an antidote called DIGIFab, or digibind, which can thankfully also be used in cases of foxglove poisoning. In the end, digoxin has saved thousands of lives – so the plant may be just as beneficial as it is detrimental.

FOXGLOVES THROUGH HISTORY

Due to the continued use of digoxin in medicine, there are plenty of accidental foxglove overdoses, certainly too numerous to mention here. There are also a fairly high number of homicides that use foxglove (or more commonly, digoxin) as a weapon of choice. Since there are so many to list, however, it makes sense to explore two of the most notorious, yet perhaps unknown cases in history.

Vincent's yellow period

It is well known to most that the world-renowned Dutch painter, Vincent van Gogh, struggled with mental health issues throughout his life. One aspect of his health that is often overlooked, however, is his struggle with seizures. These were either due to epilepsy or, as some art historians believe, his tendency to drink absinthe to excess while starving himself. Either way, these seizures played a significant part in his life, and his friend and physician Dr Gachet treated the painter's problem with a variety of medications, including digitoxin, derived from foxgloves.

While Van Gogh's treatment with foxgloves likely did very little to cure his suspected epilepsy, many art historians believe the medicine had a significant impact on the work he produced later on in his life. Xanthopsia (the effect of a yellow filter in one's vision) is a lesser-known side effect of long-term digitoxin consumption, and this is perhaps the reason behind the artist's 'yellow period', in which many of his paintings took on a yellowish hue. In the first version of the painting *Portrait of Dr Gachet* (1890), Van Gogh painted his physician with yellow skin, sitting with a foxglove flower. Likewise, in one of his most iconic works, *The Starry Night* (1899), both the moon and the stars are surrounded by yellow halos – a now well-known visual side-effect of long-term digitoxin use.

Van Gogh's subtle connection to the foxglove serves as a reminder of the complex relationship between humans and flowers, and the ways in which they can intersect in unexpected and often beautiful ways.

The murderous nurse

Charles Edmund Cullen might be America's most prolific serial killer. He is known to have murdered at least 29 people, but many suspect the death toll could be in the hundreds. Alongside lethal doses of insulin, Cullen reportedly used digoxin, derived from foxgloves, as his weapon of choice.

Cullen was born in 1960 in New Jersey, and, after a miserable high-school career, joined the US Navy. After a six-year stint, he was medically discharged for undisclosed reasons and subsequently enrolled in nursing school. He graduated in 1986, after which he started work at Saint Barnabas Medical Center in Livingstone, NJ.

In 1988, only two years after he began working as a nurse at Saint Barnabas, Cullen took his first life by administering a lethal dose of undisclosed medication to a patient intravenously. He worked at the hospital for a total of six years and it is thought that during this time, the nurse murdered as many as 12 patients using lethal doses of insulin.

In 1992, when hospital officials became suspicious of the rise in deaths at the medical centre, Cullen resigned and began working at Warren Hospital in Phillipsburg, NJ, where he took the lives of three elderly patients using what would become his preferred drug – digoxin.

Over the course of 16 years, Cullen's killing spree spanned nine hospitals and more than 40 victims. It finally ended in 2003, when officials at Somerset Medical Center noticed the strange string of deaths linked to the nurse and notified the authorities. Upon investigation, the police discovered Cullen's crimes. He was finally arrested in December 2003 and sentenced to 11 consecutive life sentences.

Lily of the Valley

Native Locations
Europe, Asia and
North America

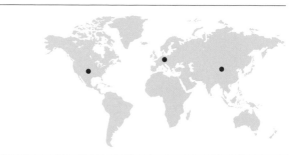

Lily of the valley (*Convallaria majus*) is a delicate and fragrant flower native to many parts of Europe, Asia and North America. In floriography, it represents purity, humility and happiness, and this is perhaps the reason that it is so often included in wedding bouquets – in fact, it is a traditional and popular addition to royal wedding flowers throughout the world.

The botanical name for the plant comes from a combination of descriptive Latin and Greek words – *convallis*, meaning 'valley'; *leiron*, meaning 'lily'; and *majalis*, meaning 'May'. So, an approximate translation of the name might be 'lily growing in the valley in May', which is exactly what the plant is.

MODE OF POISONING

Lily of the valley may seem like an innocent plant, with its delicate flowers and joyful associations, but in reality, the entire plant, including the leaves, the bulb and its flowers, is deadly. The primary cause of its toxicity is the organic compounds known as cardiac glycosides that it contains, which we previously discussed in the section on foxgloves (page 100). However, it's important to note that the term 'cardiac glycoside' is quite broad.

Lily of the valley contains an entirely different set of these compounds to foxgloves, with over 30 deadly cardiac glycosides present in the plant. Most of these are rarely found outside of lily of the valley, which is why many of them have been named after the plant. The most well-known of these compounds is convallatoxin, which has a similar effect on the human body to digoxin. Other deadly glycosides present within the plant include convallamarin, convallotoxoloside and convalloside – all of which share the prefix 'convall', which is derived from the plant's genus, *Convallarius*.

As well as a range of glycosides, lily of the valley contains other unique damaging compounds, including the amino acid 'Azetidine-2-carboxylic acid' (mercifully shortened to Aze), which is highly toxic even in very small doses. Aze can also be found in Solomon's seal (*Polygonatum*) and in some species of inedible beetroot (*Beta*), but is most prevalent in lily of the valley.

If ingested, Aze has catastrophic effects, altering the body's collagen (a protein responsible for skin elasticity), keratin (which forms the tissue responsible for growing hair, nails and the outer layer of our skin), haemoglobin (the protein that allows your blood to carry oxygen) and protein folding (necessary for proteins to become active) on a molecular level. Although little research has been conducted on the effects of Aze in humans, some studies have found that the amino acid causes severe malformations in hamsters, ducks, mice and rabbits.

While the similarities between lily of the valley poisoning and foxglove poisoning make the two difficult to tell apart, there is one set of symptoms that is present in the former that is less common in the latter. When picking foxgloves, it is of course important to proceed with caution, but skin contact will rarely cause much more than a little irritation. Lily of the valley, on the other hand, can cause severe skin irritation, and symptoms such as rashes, swelling, blistering and bumps can be observed after contact with the sap. If this is the effect the plant has on the skin, one can only imagine what havoc ingestion would wreak on our insides.

Another distinguishable difference is the presence of saponins within lily of the valley. Saponins are a type of glycoside that cause foaming when mixed with water, and many saponins derived from non-toxic plants are often used in soaps, detergents and fire extinguishers. The saponins contained in lily of the valley, however, cause extreme gastrointestinal upset – it is these compounds, rather than the cardiac glycosides within the plant, that are responsible for the nauseous symptoms that a person or animal poisoned by the plant would experience.

A SMELL SO SWEET

One of the characteristics of lily of the valley that makes it so unassuming as a deadly poison is the sweet smell omitted by the flowers. While many perfumers have attempted to extract the scent, all have failed. Even when using modern and (usually) successful distillation processes, perfumers found that instead of the sweet-smelling essential oil they so desperately sought, lily of the valley refused to produce anything other than a foul and undesirable scent.

The reason that the scent of lily of the valley is impossible to extract is because the plant produces what are known as 'mute flowers'. Mute flowers do produce scent, but only in situ – their extraction yield is non-existent and no essential oils can be made from the flowers. Perfumers first coined the term 'mute flower' in the 18th century when they were frustrated at the impossibility of extracting scent. They believed that the flowers were refusing to give up their secrets, and this term is still used to describe flowers that cannot yield essential oils.

The reason that the scent cannot be captured when the flower is distilled is simply because the flower itself does not store the scent; but instead the beguiling smell is only produced at its point of release. This means that all perfumes, soaps and air fresheners claiming to smell like lily of the valley are synthetic, and can only be made using an amalgamation of different scents to recreate what can be perceived as the smell of the true flower.

While this may be endlessly frustrating for perfumers, perhaps it is not such a bad thing after all. When one Spanish perfumer successfully managed to extract some semblance of sweet-smelling oil from the flower, it soon became clear that too many of the toxic glycosides that reside within the plant remained, which of course would elicit an extremely undesirable reaction from the wearer.

LILY OF THE VALLEY POISONINGS THROUGH HISTORY

While deaths due to lily of the valley poisoning aren't well recorded, there are incidences in which mistaken identity has caused significant damage to those unfortunate enough to consume the plant.

In many cases, poisoning occurs when curious children, left unattended, take a bite of the sumptuous-looking, bright red berries, which are present from summer onwards. Still more cases of poisoning occur when another unassuming and very forageable plant is thrown into the mix.

Wild garlic (*Allium ursinum*) is a popular culinary plant that can often be found growing in the same conditions as lily of the valley. The leaves and flowers of both plants look incredibly similar to the untrained eye. As such, cases of poisoning in adults have generally occurred when the two plants have been mixed up, or when leaves of lily of the valley have been accidentally included in the yield when foraging for wild garlic. One potential reason that records of lily of the valley poisoning are so few and far between is that wild garlic has such a small foraging window – the plant appears in early March and dies back by early June. This means that cases of mistaken identity only really happen during the time that wild garlic is available to harvest in the wild.

However, these cases are not entirely unheard of. One such instance occurred in 2013, when an unfortunate Hungarian boxing coach fell victim to the lookalikes. The 50-year-old, who had been out foraging for his favourite omelette additive one Saturday, began complaining to his son of stomach cramps and pain soon after enjoying his protein-packed dinner. The following day, his son found him dead in his apartment, and the cause of his demise was confirmed as lily of the valley.

"…Alike her ideal flower,
With its honey-laden breath,
Still her heart blooms
forth its beauty
In the valley shades
of death."

—

Paul Laurence Dunbar,
writer

CHAPTER 6

EDIBLE
BOUQUET

Spring

Many of our favourite spring flowers, such as narcissi, ranunculus, anemones and hellebores, are toxic when eaten – not particularly helpful when it comes to creating an edible bouquet! But fear not, there are a handful of beautiful edible spring flowers to pick from and plenty of recipe ideas for how to use them, too. Hopefully you will feel inspired to cook from your spring garden or dried petal pantry.

LILACS

Lilac is a shrubby bush that's blooming heralds the start of spring. Its exploding mass of delicate petals adorn the gardens of many during this joyous transition of seasons, with flowers in shades of white, pink and purple and an overall appearance not dissimilar to a hyacinth or hydrangea. Our favourite for bouquets has to be *Syringa* × *hyacinthiflora* 'Maiden's Blush', a particularly bushy variety with petals in a mix of dark pink, peachy pink and white. If you're using lilac to cook with, it might be more exciting to opt for a deep purple variety to add an unusual pop of colour to your dish.

The floral but slightly citrussy fragrance of lilac translates into a unique flavour, making it a popular choice for accenting desserts and sweet dishes. It's most common use in cooking is to infuse cordials, jams and jellies, but it can be used to flavour milks and cream, too. Maddie is an avid posset-maker, and we think a lilac posset or rice pudding would be quite delicious – though you might want to opt for lighter-coloured flowers.

While the purple could be off-putting in some recipes, it would be perfect for dusting over baked goods. Try blending dried lilac petals with granulated sugar and sifting this vibrant mix over freshly fried doughnuts or warm shortbread. Not only will the colour pep up

an otherwise beige biscuit (cookie), but the uniquely citrussy floral flavour will bring some zing to your bake.

PANSIES AND VIOLETS

Pansies (*Viola* × *wittrockiana*) are one of the most attractive edible flowers, but unfortunately they have very little flavour. Even so, they can still bring plenty to a dish. We have all heard the phrase 'eating with your eyes' when referring to a plate of food that gets the tastebuds tingling just by looking at it, and the small but fierce pansy does just that. Their dark centres and bold-hued edges make a dish look so inviting that they are one of the most favoured ways to garnish a plate. While the petals alone are extremely mild in flavour, if you eat the whole flower (sepals and all) you will discover an earthy flavour reminiscent of winter greens that works perfectly as an accompaniment to both light spring salads and rich, hearty meat dishes.

Violets, the flowers from which pansies were derived, on the other hand, can be used as a cooking ingredient as well as a garnish. They may not be as varied in appearance as pansies, but their attractive purple and blue petals are a classic sign of spring. As a garnish, they're often paired with cheese and fruit or used to dress salads, desserts and drinks. Their most common use, however, is in making sweet treats. If you've never tasted a violet, you might be able to conjure up an idea of their flavour from the old-fashioned sweets (candies) 'Parma Violets'. Although these are an acquired taste, the flavour of the flower itself is much more gentle. Like lilac, the dried petals of violets can be blended with sugar to create a subtle violet-flavoured dusting for biscuits and cakes. The very best way to make use of their striking colour, though, is in syrups and frostings. Violet syrup is a marvellous addition to cocktails and lemonade, with its electric blue hue and subtle berry-like flavour. The syrup can then also be used to make frosting for cupcakes. A versatile little flower indeed, and certainly not one to be overlooked.

BORAGE

This late spring flower is one you might well have eaten before. The leaves, stalks and flowers of borage (*Borago officinalis*), also known as starflower, are all edible and share a cucumber-like flavour that is ideal for using in salads. In the UK, its most common use is as a garnish for one of the nation's favourite fair-weather drinks, Pimms. Try adding a few leaves to a jug (pitcher) of Pimms, along with your favourite late spring or early summer berries and fruits. We like to pop a few of the flowers in an ice cube tray to make floral ice to add to a gin and tonic. It can also be brewed to make a light and refreshing tea. It's not just drinks that borage is good for, though. Its foliage can be used in hot savoury dishes such as soups, stocks and stews, where it should be treated like any other fresh herb. Try mixing borage leaves with ricotta to fill homemade ravioli – serve with lots of butter and freshly grated nutmeg. Delicious!

MARIGOLDS

Marigolds (*Tagetes*) are late spring flowers that are favoured in cottage gardens. Their richly coloured frill of petals helps to attract pollinating insects, so they're often used as a companion plant, the name given to a plant grown in close proximity to another to provide benefits such as pest protection or to increase crop productivity.

Only the petals of marigolds are used in cooking, and their flavour varies wildly between varieties, from citrussy to spicy and tangy to peppery, making them a versatile ingredient across both sweet and savoury dishes. The deeply saturated, orange, yellow and red petals are good for more than just flavour, though. They are a great way to add some rich colour to a salad, and, when heated, their colour will transfer on to paler ingredients around them, making them a great substitute for saffron. Try chopping and sautéing marigold petals in stir-fries and curries in the same way you would a herb to add both flavour and colour to the dish.

Summer

There are so many edible summer flowers that we had to whittle down the selection to just a few of our favourites that we've used most frequently over the years. The light, fresh and sweet flavours of summer flower petals tend to lend themselves to sweet dishes, teas and cordials, but there are a few exceptions, including the florist's favourite, alliums.

ALLIUMS

The genus *Allium* contains well-known kitchen staples, including garlic, onions, leeks, chives, spring onions (scallions) and the forager's favourite, wild garlic (ramsons). The plants grown for their flowers (known commonly as alliums or ornamental onions) have incredibly flavourful florets (small flowers), which are found in abundance on the flower head, usually in shades of bright, summery purple but occasionally white. Depending on the variety, the flavours will range from bold and pungent to a more delicate oniony taste, but always with enough flavour to warrant their place on a plate. Although others in their genus are ideal for cooking, alliums are not. Use them instead to finish pastas, risottos and potato salads. In fact, you can use them in any dish in which you might opt for the more delicate flavour of chives as a garnish instead of raw garlic or onion.

On a trip to your local flower shop, there will probably be a few varieties of allium available over the summer months. Some with small, bullet-like heads similar to those you'd find on a chive, others with dramatically large bursts of purple flowers on top of long, thick stems. The variety you are most likely to see is *Allium hollandicum* 'Purple Sensation', which is regularly found dotted through the borders of early summer gardens. Their statuesque, globe-shaped

flowers tower above the other early summer blooms, and the dense mass of super-vibrant florets makes them the perfect choice for those looking to use them in food.

HONEYSUCKLE

In a typical English country garden, there is likely to be a honey-suckle (*Lonicera*) scrambling up a trellis alongside the alliums. Honeysuckle climbs like a jasmine (*Jasminum officinale*), and although it has flowers in abundance, it is predominantly made up of leafy green foliage. It's the highly fragrant and colourful tubular flowers, however, that house the sweet nectar we are searching for to make our edible bouquet. Both the flowers and nectar are safe to eat and can be consumed straight from the plant – try sucking on a flower for a honey-like hit of sugar. Take care to avoid the berries, though, as some varieties may be toxic.

In the culinary world, honeysuckle is most often used to make tea or a sweet and flavourful syrup. You can use the syrup to sweeten ice tea, lemonade, yoghurt and sorbet. Think of it as a more floral-tasting honey substitute. The flowers, with their intoxicating scent and yellow and pink pastel hues, work fantastically as an edible garnish on savoury foods, too. They can have a bitter undertone if the calyx (the green part at the base of each trumpet) isn't removed, but it's not a necessity and can add a welcome layer of sour flavour to salads, which might otherwise come from vinegar or lemon in a dressing. This bitterness also works well for infusing alcohol such as gin and vodka, but be sure to use only the sweet nectar if making sweet wines or mead.

CARNATIONS

The biggest clue as to how carnations (*Dianthus caryophyllus*) taste is their perfumed aroma, in particular that of the old-fashioned cottage garden pinks. The petals are a little peppery with a hint of clove or nutmeg, giving them a sweet-but-spicy flavour that works wonderfully in savoury and sweet dishes. Carnations are one of the ingredients used in the French herbal liqueur chartreuse, and they make a great addition to other spirits and cocktails as well. You can infuse alcohol directly by mixing it with the carnation petals and then leaving the mixture to steep for a few weeks, or you can make a carnation syrup to be added to cocktails for a sweeter flavour profile. Simply pour boiling water over the petals and leave them to flavour the water before mixing with sugar and reducing to a syrup over a low heat.

In cooking, carnations are most commonly sautéed with meat and vegetables or used as a seasoning for fried rice dishes. If using carnations straight from the garden, be sure to cut the petals away from the bitter-tasting white base of the flower that connects it to the stem, and remove the stamen and sepals too. Try finely chopping the petals with other seasonal herbs and frying them in butter over a low heat to pour over ravioli or tortellini.

CHAMOMILE

Chamomile (*Chamaemelum nobile* and *Matricaria chamomilla*) is a daisy-like flower that is one of the most ancient medicinal herbs known to mankind and is well known for its use in tea. It is credited with a wide variety of health and wellness benefits, from improving sleep and soothing nerves to comforting teething babies, and historically it has been used to treat an extensive list of human ailments including gastrointestinal disorders, ulcers and even haemorrhoids. In food, however, it's famed for its subtle, floral flavour, which lends itself to light puddings. The calming and delicately sweet chamomile flower has an almost apple-like flavour. Try drying chamomile and infusing the petals into a cheesecake or ice cream base to make the most of the floral taste. It is great in jams and jellies, too, either mixed with other delicate flavours or as the star of the show in sponge and cream cakes and meringues.

SCENTED GERANIUMS
AND ROSE PETALS

Roses and geraniums are used to flavour foods across the world, particularly sweets and puddings. Geraniums have a much broader flavour spectrum, ranging from citrus and spice to fruits and flowers, the taste generally corresponding to the variety (rose geraniums have a rose-like flavour, for example, and lemon geraniums have a lemon-flavoured flower). Both the petals and stems of the geranium are edible, but the prickly texture of the leaf means this part of the plant is more commonly used to infuse liquids, while the petals are eaten directly. The bright pastel colours, usually shades of pink, yellow and red, add a sweet and delicate touch when sprinkled over sponge cakes and give a tangy sharpness to creamy deserts. Try making a syrup or cordial with the foliage of different varieties to make geranium lemonade, or freeze the petals into ice cubes for a pretty summer party drink.

Roses are an even more common ingredient than geraniums. Their flavour is used a lot in Middle Eastern cooking, both sweet and savoury, but it is a baking staple in many other territories, too. You're likely to find dried rose petals or rose water in large supermarkets (grocery stores), but all roses are edible, so you can just as easily use flowers from your garden or ones that you've foraged. Petals can be sugared or crystallised to dress cupcakes, cheesecakes or brownies, and you can freeze them in ice cubes for punches and cocktails, just like geranium petals. Their most common use is in jams, jellies and syrups, with Turkish delight probably taking the top spot as the most famous rose-flavoured food. Rose cordial in a gin cocktail is one of our favourite ways to enjoy their bright and floral taste.

"Flowers are not typically found in everyday meals, so their deliberate inclusion in a dish makes that dish something special, a treat for the receiver."

—

Constance Kirker,
Edible Flowers: A Global History

Autumn

Unlike summer, the edible flowers of autumn (fall) lend themselves much better to savoury recipes, which feels appropriate, as these are the foods we tend to want to eat as the weather starts to cool. There are plenty of flowers you can eat at this time of year, many of which are familiar favourites, and there are lots of classic and new ways of cooking with them, too.

NASTURTIUMS

Though not as commonly used as a cut flower, nasturtiums (*Tropaeolum*) must be mentioned when discussing edible flowers. Their brightly coloured blossoms and unique, savoury flavour have secured the plant's place as a firm culinary favourite. Nasturtiums flower right through summer and autumn, so you'll get plenty of use from this versatile plant, in cooking as well as seasonal bouquets. Both the leaves and flowers are edible and can be eaten cooked or raw. They have a peppery and slightly spicy flavour profile, with the blossoms having a lighter and more delicate taste than the leaves, making them better suited to garnishing sweet dishes such as cakes and pastries.

The funnel-shaped flowers of nasturtiums are typically bright orange, red or yellow, and are a beautiful garnish for most dishes. Use the round, lily-pad-shaped leaves in the base of a salad and dress it with the flowers to create a feast for the eyes as well as the tastebuds. For an extra tangy kick, you can pickle the flower buds just like capers. Try blending the leaves into a pesto with nuts, oil and Parmesan to go with pasta, and use both pickled and fresh flowers to dress it.

SUNFLOWERS

You may think sunflowers (*Helianthus annuus*) are an obvious choice. We all know that sunflower seeds and the cooking oil made from them are widely available and regularly used. But you might not be aware that you can also eat the petals and even the flower buds, too. The buds can be steamed and eaten like artichokes, and they have a similar tart, vegetable taste, though slightly more bitter. Try dipping them into aioli to counteract the bitter edge. If you grow sunflowers, it might become an autumn recipe staple.

The sunshine-coloured petals have a faintly bittersweet flavour and are more widely available than the buds, so if you're not growing your own sunflowers, this might be the way to go. They can be dried and used in autumn salads for a touch of vibrancy, or sprinkled on to a tray of autumnal vegetables as a seasoning, much like the petals of chrysanthemums or carnations.

If you do end up growing sunflowers in your garden, make sure to harvest the seeds at the end of the season as they make fantastic microgreens. Gather the seeds and soak them before sprinkling over a shallow seed tray filled with compost. Water the surface of the compost and then cover the tray with cardboard to keep the seeds damp and in darkness. After three or four days, remove the cardboard, and you should see small sprouts have shot up. Leave uncovered to grow for a further seven days, and then you can start snipping and harvesting as you like to use in salads or as a garnish.

CHRYSANTHEMUMS

Chrysanthemum flowers can differ considerably in taste – some are hot and peppery, some are sweeter and some even have a mild cauliflower flavour. In fact, there are thousands of varieties of chrysanthemum, all of which have edible flowers, so it's best to take a nibble of a few different ones to find out which you enjoy.

The petals should be blanched before they're added to fresh dishes, but they can also be dried to use all year round, as can the buds, which are often used in East Asian countries to make tea. The buds have a strong, earthy flavour that's unique but very refreshing, and is perfect in a hot and humid country. We use dried buds to flavour vinegar, which works fantastically for pickling onions and cabbage to tone down the acidity.

The fresh petals are perfect for roasting with vegetables and tossing into salads. The vibrant mix of colours available will liven up any plate – mix and match and go for an autumnal rainbow. Much like carnations, you should remove the white flower base, as it's very bitter. If you're growing *Glebionis coronaria*, also known as crown daisy, then you can make use of the leaves, too. They're known as 'chrysanthemum greens' and are widely used in stir fries and steamed vegetable dishes.

PHYSALIS

Physalis (*Physalis peruviana*), also known as cape gooseberry, are a long-standing favourite of ours. We have strong memories of sneaking stems from the display in our mum's flower shop and nibbling on the berries. As a cut flower, they have a tall stem with edible berries encased in what look like orange paper lanterns running its length. While they're a popular flower throughout the season, they really come into their own around Halloween, when they sit perfectly alongside carved pumpkins and decorative gourds.

The berry, which bears a strong resemblance to a tomatillo, but orange in colour, has a tartness that's ideal for pairing with sweets. They are most commonly eaten raw, as a garnish to rich and chocolatey dishes, or as a stand-alone canapé after being dipped in chocolate. The papery lantern is often left attached for decoration, as when it has dried it will keep its orange colour, but the beautiful, silvery veins start to surface, too, much like a dried leaf.

Physalis berries can be cooked and are wonderful baked into sweet muffins or made into jam. Try swapping strawberry jam for physalis in a sponge cake if you prefer something less sweet. Or make a jelly to be paired with fatty meats in place of cranberry sauce. We like to add raw berries to a smoothie or fruit salad, as they're a great source of vitamin C and have antioxidant properties, too.

"There is free food all around us."

—

Ava Chin,
Author of *Eating Wildly*

CHAPTER 7

FLOWERS FOR SALE AND THE DUTCH MARKET

Having had a foot in the flower industry for much of our lives, we are no strangers to selling this popular product. But receiving deliveries of fresh flowers from our Dutch wholesalers overnight means that we are rarely thinking about how these flowers made it to us in the first place.

Although we had read about the Dutch flower industry online and in articles, we decided that the best way to explore it's inner workings was by seeing it for ourselves. Doing this meant we could pass our experiences on to you from our unique perspective.

During our visit to the Netherlands, we had the great pleasure of being shown the ins and outs of the industry by those working within it. We visited cut-flower growers, auction houses and wholesalers to get a rounded view of flower production from start to finish. We hope this gives you a good understanding of just how much effort goes into the flowers that end up in your home.

THE GROWERS

The sheer scale of the flower-growing industry in Holland is breath-taking, and after visiting just a few of the businesses growing under glass there, it is clear why the Dutch growers hold the unchallenged title as leaders in the field. There have been quite a few challenges for the growers in the Netherlands in recent years, including Covid-19, the energy crisis and undertaking the changes necessary to becoming a more sustainable industry. But touring the glasshouses ourselves, we witnessed some of the many innovative ways in which the people running them have faced up to these challenges and begun to tackle them head-on.

Driving through Rijnsburg, a village in the western Netherlands, it seems that about a third of the town is dedicated to the flower industry, with a section at the northernmost point made up entirely of greenhouses. This is where the two flower growers we visited, Dutch Lily Masters and Esmeralda, are located. On the way through Rijnsburg we passed the Royal FloraHolland auction, one of the three main flower auction houses in The Netherlands, where many of the flowers we saw would end up in the early hours of the next morning.

DUTCH LILY MASTERS

We arrive at Dutch Lily Masters after a short tour through a sea of glasshouses, and meet one of the company's sales team, who will show us around. The growing systems here are mostly automated now, a move made in 2003 in order to prevent wastage and save on staffing (they previously needed about 30 members of staff to check, water and cut the crops). Because of this, we are greeted by a wall of lilies that is taller than us, moving steadily in our direction. It almost feels like stepping into the future, though perhaps this just shows how dated our preconceptions about how flowers are grown and harvested are.

The lilies are grown in shallow trays that sit on moving tables, which are mounted on a series of tracks leading to the cutting room. There are about 100 rows of tables in the glasshouse and 10,000 lilies per row – quite a sight to see, and their sweet-but-spicy scent in such epic quantities is almost overpowering. Each morning, the sea of lilies is looked over row by row via camera. Tables with lilies ready for cutting are selected and moved inside automatically using the tracks. They are met by two workers, who harvest any ripe stems before sending the plants that aren't quite ready back out to the glasshouse; they are sprayed with water and nutrients on their way. Cut stems are placed individually on to a conveyor belt that takes them to a small team of packers, who check each stem and group them into tens for wrapping. This process of cutting and wrapping with little human contact saves on huge numbers of stem breakages, a common problem when the lilies were being cut in the glasshouses and carried over the shoulders of workers to the packing stations. The reduction of waste from breakages not only helps with the grower's profit margins but is also more environmentally friendly, as the water and energy that go into growing each stem aren't wasted.

Automation isn't the only way Dutch Lily Masters is reducing its waste. Although each lily bulb can only be used once, they are steamed and composted to be used again in a new form, helping the next generation of plants to grow. In fact, it's not only the bulbs that are steam-cleaned, but the soil that housed them, too. Once processed, it is mixed in equal parts with fresh soil (including some of the composted bulbs), which provides the much-needed nutrients that the steamed soil no longer has. This recycling of soil means that even though the compost is not necessarily peat-free (a big concern in the sustainability of the plant and flower industry), it is at least used many times, and the amount of 'new' growing medium used has dropped by about two-thirds.

We leave Dutch Lily Masters with a new-found appreciation of lilies, having been introduced to some of the company's more unusual varieties on our way out. These varieties are growing in popularity

and helping the sometimes-overlooked lily make its comeback with the flower buyers of our generation.

ESMERELDA

Our next visit is with Esmerelda, a company that focuses on growing gerberas. This flower is often associated with supermarket (grocery store) flowers in the UK, but it is slowly but surely making its way back into the displays of trendy flower shops across the nation. Although they haven't been at the forefront of flower trends in the UK, their popularity doesn't seem to have taken a hit in Europe.

It's only a two-minute drive between the two growers, and we are transported quickly from an awesome sea of green to a vast show of colour – gerberas in hot pink, vibrant yellow, burnt orange, bright red and pastel peach fill this 4-hectare (10-acre) glasshouse. Our guide from Esmerelda tells us that germinis (a smaller type of gerbera with a head under 9 cm/2 inches) are currently the most popular and take up three-quarters of the glasshouse. Although it's the colour of the flowers that is most arresting, there is an added element of psychedelic surrealness coming from the lights. Every couple of metres, there is a pink or yellow light shining down on the plants, alternating in colour along the rows. The bright pink lights are LED – a relatively new introduction to the glasshouses. They're much more energy-efficient and provide a decent enough amount of light to encourage healthy growth in the plants. However, the use of sodium lights (the yellow lights) is still a necessity here. Although they use about three times more energy than their LED counterparts, they also up the temperature in the glasshouse by about 8°C (14°F), a temperature increase that in times of struggle with heating costs is incredibly valuable. We are told that when using only LED lights, the quality of the flowers has been found to drop significantly.

As we walk down the rows of plants, we notice that each plant has its own pot, unlike the trays full of lilies we have just seen. One of the reasons for this is that each plant is used for about three years before it's replaced, flowering continuously in that time, with the growers being able to harvest flowers from a single plant every other day. It's important that each plant has enough water and nutrients without competing with its neighbours, so each pot has its own water irrigation system. Any excess water not used by the plant drips into a pipe running below the rows of pots and travels to a tank where it's cleaned with UV light before being reused on the crops – a fantastic way to use and recycle resources. Esmerelda also use a ground-source heat pump below the glasshouses to raise the temperature inside.

We make our way out of the warm and slightly trippy-feeling grow rooms and back into the packing area, where the flowers harvested earlier that day are now packed up and ready to leave. The larger gerberas are hung in cardboard boxes with individual slots for each flower to protect their heads, their stems dangling into a pool of fresh water until they're loaded on to lorries. Trolleys full of germinis are lined up beside the pools. Esmerelda now sells through the auction and direct to wholesaler in equal measure, so half the trolleys are already allocated to buyers and ready to be collected. The rest we will see again at the Rijnsburg auction in the morning.

THE AUCTION

We set off for Royal FloraHolland Rijnsburg at 5.30 a.m. Although this feels early to us, it is considered a late start for regular attendees, who usually arrive at about 4 a.m. The roads feel surprisingly busy, but we remind ourselves that the area's core workforce is part of the flower industry and most of these people are travelling to or from the auction.

We'd heard tales of these auctions from our Dutch opa and mum (who had visited the auction with him on a few occasions as a child), so we had ideas of what it might be like prior to our arrival, but as with our trip to the glasshouses, we found our preconceptions to be dated. Although we weren't expecting an auction room hazy with cigarette smoke and buyers shouting at the auctioneer, we also weren't expecting to be met with an almost empty room.

Bidding is now done online so there isn't much need to work on site, and tuning in to the auction remotely is actually much more efficient, as buyers can look at stock across all three of the main auctions at once. That's not to say they don't visit the auction houses at all – in fact, most buyers will be up long before dawn to see the stock on offer in real life, checking the quality but also getting an idea of size, weight and height. At the stock room, buyers can scan trolleys of flowers they're particularly interested in and receive an alert when these flowers pop up on the auction screens. Having seen and checked the flower stock, the vast majority of buyers will head back to their offices, from where they can tune in live to the auctions for a 6 a.m. start.

THE FLOWERS FOR SALE

As soon as we arrive, we are ushered downstairs to look at the stock along with the wholesalers before the auction begins. Although we won't be buying, it's amazing to get an idea of how many different grades, colours and heights of each flower are available. As well as wholesale buyers checking the quality of the stock, there are auction workers doing the same to ensure the growers have correctly registered the weight and quality of their harvest before it goes live. Any flowers they consider to have been registered incorrectly will not go on sale until they have been re-evaluated by both the grower and the auction house.

Choosing a few different grades of each flower is also an important a part of the process for the buyers. Wholesalers generally like to offer the same flower in a range of different prices and sizes to suit their customers' needs, so picking out a well-rounded offering prior to the auction is key.

In the rooms below the bidding space, we see aisles and aisles of beautiful spring flowers: ranunculus, hyacinths, tulips and anemones, patiently waiting to be loaded on to the first bidders' lorries. But as we journey through, we are surprised to see a whole room full to the brim with varieties you wouldn't expect to see in early spring – delphiniums, alliums, scabious and scented stocks, to name a few. Many of the most popular flowers are now being grown all year round by Dutch growers who have upped sticks and followed the sun, setting up nurseries around the world, most commonly in Africa, Portugal and Israel. Some 'all year round' varieties are relatively new to the scene and still surprising to find them outside of their natural season, others have been available as such for so long now that it doesn't feel strange at all to buy them throughout the year – snapdragons, clematis and chrysanthemums are just a few examples.

Walking among these summer flowers in February, we realise that the auctions are selling flowers not only from local growers, such as the gerberas from Esmerelda we'd seen being cut the day before, but from growers all over the world. It's then that it hits us just how many of the world's flowers come through the Dutch auctions before being shipped back out across Europe.

THE BIDDING ROOM

We get so carried away looking at the mass of flowers that we miss the 6 a.m. start and have to hurry back upstairs to the bidding room to catch as much of the action as possible – this is, after all, the main event.

The room itself is like an auditorium. Rows of tables with bidding buttons from the pre-internet days of the auction are stepped above each other and a stage at the front sits below a row of massive screens. They used to parade trolleys of flowers on to the stage for show while the auctioneer provided information about them in a melodic (but to some almost incomprehensible) manner. Now the stage is empty, and the auctioneer speaks directly to buyers' headsets, whether they're remote or in the room itself. He is providing information about where flowers are grown, who grew them and what's coming up next on the screens. We can't hear what's being said, but we enjoy listening to the whooping and oohs and aahs that the buyers let out in response.

On the screens, there is a lot to look at in a short amount of time. The screens are mostly taken up by a large clock-like circle, but instead of telling the time, it relays amounts of money. The clock starts at €1 (about £0.90/$1), in the 12 o'clock position, and works anti-clockwise down to 0. That's right, the Dutch flower auctions (unlike any other auction) go backwards in a sort of flower-based game of chicken. The price per stem starts at the maximum the buyers and auctioneers think it could sell for and then a red dot starts to move anti-clockwise, going down in price until someone bids. It's certainly a test of nerve – if a bucket or trolley of flowers comes up that you know you need, you must wait until it gets to what you deem a reasonable price before placing your bid, all the while hoping that someone else doesn't stop the clock first. As soon as someone bids, the red dot stops on the clock, the next flower appears, and the dot flies back to its starting position.

While that may sound fairly simple, the clock isn't all there is to see on the screens. For every new flower that appears, a whole host of new information is provided – the quantity of stems you're bidding on, stem length, ripeness/openness and, for some flowers, the number of buds per stem. It also lets you know how many more opportunities there will be to bid on this variety of flower, so the buyer can assess how risky they can be with their bidding. The fewer chances to buy a flower there are left, the higher the price at which the bids stop.

Another factor that comes into play for the more expensive flowers is the price multiplication. The clock's maximum price is €1 but there are certain stems, such as hydrangeas, that will sell for more. For these flowers, there is a box that states how many times to multiply the price by. Most of the time this box will say 1c, indicating that the starting price is €1, but during our time in the auction room, we see it move to 3c for a particularly tall and striking variety of *Fritillaria*, telling us that the bid was starting at €3.

You can imagine how hard this job is. The buyers must digest all the necessary information in the split second before the clock starts its backward decline, then hold off for as long as is bearable before the pressure of losing the bid becomes too great, and only then hit the button before the process starts again.

Luckily, there are many tricks of the trade that make bidding easier for those experienced buyers on the front line. Letters on their keyboards correspond to numbers from 1 to 18, so if they want 14 buckets of ranunculus, they don't need to waste time hitting two keys. Knowing the auctioneer starts with the tallest stems and finishes with the shortest also means they can make an educated guess at stem length without have to check the box. There are many other tips and tricks offered up to us, but even these shortcuts are a lot for us to take in as auction novices.

Large wholesalers will have a team of buyers to do their bidding. The load is split between a group in which each person has their own speciality – rose buyer, seasonal flower buyer, chrysanthemum buyer and so on. Each person's expert knowledge of specific flowers, their growers and how they've sold each day at auction is invaluable.

This guides them on how much they should be bidding and varieties or growers to avoid. They will also take into account their customers' feedback, and advice from marketing teams on which flowers are most sought after at the time.

Having spent a solid chunk of time getting sucked into the thrill of the auction and its hypnotic backwards clocks, we head to our wholesaler's HQ to visit their buying team and find out where the flowers they've bought go from here.

WHOLESALE

At the headquarters of our wholesaler, Van der Plas, we meet Henk, the grandson of Willem Van Der Plas, who founded the company in 1970. Henk now runs the show, along with his father and uncles. Their business has grown exponentially in recent years, and we are told how one 'lazy uncle' set the cogs of change turning, resulting in the ultra-efficiency of the company today.

Henk's father and his brothers entered the business in 1986 as 'Flying Dutchmen', the name given to wholesalers who would hit the road with flower-filled trucks, selling to retailers across the continent. While this life on the move was common for many sellers in the industry, it wasn't easy going. They'd usually spend six days a week away from home, driving overnight to ensure they reached their customers with fresh flowers by early morning. Grabbing moments of sleep in the bunks above the driver's cabin was their only real rest before heading back to Holland for fresh stock and starting the journey again.

After years of doing this, one brother decided he'd had enough and that a change of lifestyle was in order – preferably to one that involved working from a desk and getting home to his family in the evenings. As this was the lifestyle he craved, he was the one tasked with making it happen. He taught himself the tech skills necessary to create an online world for the Flying Dutchmen, and in 2007, the wholesale website was born.

Fast-forward to today and all of Van der Plas's flower selling is done online. The Flying Dutchmen deal with their customers mostly over text message and telephone, only jetting off once every other month or so to visit and have a catch-up. For many other wholesalers, this change to a remote way of working only came about following the Covid-19 pandemic, making Van der Plas a true leader in its field.

THE BUYERS

When we arrive back from the auction, the buying team are still well and truly in the thick of it, their eyes glued to their own set of screens, flicking between auction houses with the click of a button. Van der Plas has eight buyers for flowers and six for plants, with three of the flower buyers tasked with picking roses. It is one of the few companies that buys most of its stock directly from the growers, so while the buyers still have plenty to source from the auction, much of their work is done before it starts.

When customer orders start flooding in, both buyers and the sales team will contact the growers with their customers' requests, getting a foot in the door before the flowers are packed up for the auction houses. Not only does this avoid the possibility of losing out at auction, it means their customers will get the freshest stock possible. Newly cut stems make their way to the Van der Plas warehouse straight from the cutting bench and leave again for the retailer later on that afternoon. Buying direct from the grower means there is only a two-day turn-around before the flowers are on display in local flower shops. In comparison, anything bought at auction will be sold the day after cutting and arrive at the wholesaler's warehouse later that morning to be photographed, organised and uploaded to the website. It will then be sent out to the final retailer over the following few days once ordered. Although it only adds a day or two to the process and these flowers will still have a long shelf-life, the fresher the flowers, the better.

Another huge positive of buying to order is the decrease in waste. Even though the Flying Dutchmen could make extremely well-educated guesses about how many flowers their customers might need, it's impossible to predict exact numbers, so they would end up selling off any excess stock cheaply, resulting in a loss of profit. If they couldn't sell it off even at a reduced rate, it would end up in the bin, now too old to sell when it reached Dutch shores once again.

GETTING TO YOU

The first of the day's trucks carrying the flowers won at auction start to arrive at around 7 a.m. Trolleys and trolleys full of flowers are whisked away for checking before they enter into a colour- and scent-filled production line. They're then sent off on conveyor belts to different locations across the warehouse before being loaded on to one of Van Der Plas's 65 trucks, which will drive across Europe to the company's retail customers.

Depending on where they were grown and if they were bought from the auction or directly from the grower, the flowers could have been cut any time between five days ago and earlier that morning. We would normally expect flowers to last a week in a vase at home, so stems being cut five days prior to sale might sound shocking. However, it is surprising just how long flowers kept in cool and dry conditions will last after they've been cut – for some flowers, it is as long as a month.

It never ceases to amaze us just how many people and how much complex work is involved in the flower industry – all for a product that although not useful, edible or a necessity in any way, is something that, as humans, we seem to need. The joy and happiness their beauty brings to our lives can be likened to the uplifting feelings we experience when listening to music and enjoying the arts. Research overwhelmingly shows the positive impact that flowers and plants have on our mental health, productivity, problem-solving and general mood, so the work, attention and care that goes into bringing us this product of natural beauty is certainly of value to us.

Glossary

Androgynophore: the column in the centre of a flower that elevates the reproductive parts of the flower.

Anther: the male, pollen-producing part of the flower.

Floriography: the Victorian language of flowers.

Filament: the thread-like stalk that supports the anther.

Coronal filament: a circle of filaments that radiates from the centre of a flower to the petals.

Nectaries: specialised glands that secrete nectar.

Operculum: a cap, lid or protective structure made from a fusion of petals.

Ovary: the part of the flower that contains ovules, which produce seeds after being fertilised.

Proboscis: the elongated, tubular, sucking mouthpart of an insect (often present in bees, butterflies and moths).

Sepals: the outer part of a flower, which serves to protect the flower while in bud.

Stigma: the sticky, pollen-receiving female part of the flower.

Style: the stalk that connects the stigma to the ovary.

Acknowledgements

We would like to say a massive thank you to everyone who has helped to make this book possible.

Firstly, to Eve and Eila at Hardie Grant, two of the most patient, helpful and enthusiastic people we could ever have dreamed of working with. Their guidance and ideas have been the backbone of all of our work, and we are truly grateful for their ongoing support and their faith in us.

We'd like to thank Stuart, our designer, whose meticulous eye is part of the reason the book is so beautiful. And to Lucy Rose, whose incredible illustrations are the other reason.

A massive thank you to Henk, Henk (no, this is not a typo) and the team at Van Der Plas who showed us the inner workings of their business, and took us on a tour of Holland and many of its greenhouses, so we could get the best all-round view of the magic behind the cut-flower industry.

We'd also like to thank Vivi (@byvivi.co) and Anastasia for all of their insight into the world of flowers in their respective home countries of Mexico and Russia. We are so grateful that you took the time to teach us.

To all of the team at Forest (Ella, Lou, Eva, Seb, Thea, Anastasia and Maya) for holding down the fort and supplying endless comedic relief and advice when the going got tough.

We'd also like to thank our family for being a such a tight unit. They have always supported and encouraged us and we are extremely lucky they're patient enough to listen to us natter on about plants, flowers, books and business all day long.

And finally, a huge thank you to our mum, Fran. Her extensive knowledge of flowers has given us the building blocks for our work, and visiting her flower farm has provided endless inspiration. Without her unwavering support, guidance and encouragement, this book might never have materialised.

About the Authors

Alice and Maddie's love of plants and flowers started at an early age. They helped their opa (a Dutch grower of cut flowers) on his nurseries and allotment, and their mum (an award-winning horticulturist) in the garden and with her cut-flower business, The Fresh Flower Company, which has been running for over 20 years. They began experimenting with indoor plants before opening their first houseplant shop, Forest, in 2013.

In 2021, they published their first book *The Green Indoors*. Following this, they created a houseplant studio with their mum and the team at Forest for the RHS's Chelsea Flower Show, and won a gold medal for their work. Most recently, in 2021, the pair published their second book *The Hidden Histories of Houseplants*, the first in the *Hidden Histories* series.

Maddie Bailey

Maddie began working at Forest in 2013 after school. Inspired by her mother's love for horticulture and the surrounding environment of both plants and cut-flowers, she began studying Horticulture with the RHS in 2015.

After finishing her studies, she continued to work both in the shop and as a gardener. During this time, she expanded her knowledge with self-study and wrote articles for her Instagram account @Muddy_Maddie. The articles combined her love for horticulture, the great outdoors, houseplants and science.

After juggling gardening and shop-work for two years, Maddie then travelled around the world to destinations such as South America, North America, the Middle East and the Arctic Circle, taking time to observe plants in different climates and paying particular attention to the plants we cultivate for indoor use.

Maddie has since been practising her fiction writing, and learning about the cultivation of cut flowers by working with her mum at the family's flower farm in the picturesque countryside of Kent.

Alice Bailey

As a teenager, Alice started working at her mum's flower shop, where her experience with flowers and plants and her eye for design grew. After leaving school, she worked for an independent lifestyle store which ignited her love of homewares, interiors and visual merchandising. During this time, she started a small company with a friend and colleague, where together they developed a more well-rounded view of business. In 2012, Alice returned to The Fresh Flower Company where, having continuously studied the growth habits of indoor plants, she and her mum Fran introduced a selection of houseplants to their customers. The decision to open Forest, a houseplant and lifestyle store, came shortly afterwards as the popularity of indoor plants increased. With their combined love of business and shared knowledge of the flower and plant industry, they, together with Maddie, evolved the business into what it is today. Since exhibiting at the Chelsea Flower show, Alice has become a member of the RHS Tender Ornamental Plant Committee, where her knowledge of plants and flowers will continue to bloom. Alongside expanding the business, Alice is hoping to inspire the next generation of green-fingered folk through her work with the RHS.

INDEX

tuberose (*Polianthes tuberosa*) 33
tuberous roots 64

U
United Kingdom. *see* Britain

V
Valentine's Day 44–5
Van der Plas 144–7
Venus 42
Vertumnus 18
Victorians and flowers 10, 13, 17, 18, 42
violets 116

W
wedding flowers 42, 106
weeds
    bindweed 62, 65–8
    controlling 52–3
    dandelion 50, 54–60
    definition of 50–2
    ecological importance 58–60, 66–8
    herbicides 52–3, 60, 66
    learning from 53
white flowers 33–4, 42
white lilies (*Lilium candidum*) 42
wholesalers 144–7
wild garlic (*Allium ursinum*) 110
witches
    and deadly nightshade 27
    and elder trees 25
Withering, William 103
wolfsbane (*Aconitum*) 27, 92–9
wood: elder trees 24–5
woodland bluebells 12–14

Y
yellow flowers: Russia 39

Z
Zantedeschia aethiopica (calla lily) 33–4
Zephyrus 13–14

Published in 2024 by Hardie Grant Books,
an imprint of Hardie Grant Publishing

Hardie Grant Books (London)
5th & 6th Floors
52–54 Southwark Street
London SE1 1UN

Hardie Grant Books (Melbourne)
Building 1, 658 Church Street
Richmond, Victoria 3121

hardiegrantbooks.com

British Library Cataloguing-in-Publication Data.
A catalogue record for this book is available from
the British Library.

The Hidden Histories of Flowers
ISBN: 978-1-78488-674-5

10 9 8 7 6 5 4 3 2 1

Publishing Director: Kajal Mistry
Commissioning Editor: Eve Marleau
Senior Editor: Eila Purvis
Design and Art Direction: Stuart Hardie
Illustrator: Lucy Rose
Copy-editor: Lucy Kingett
Proofreader: Tara O'Sullivan
Indexer: Cathy Heath
Production Controller: Martina Georgieva

Colour reproduction by p2d
Printed and bound in China by Leo Paper Products Ltd.